Hanne Darboven

Hanne Darboven

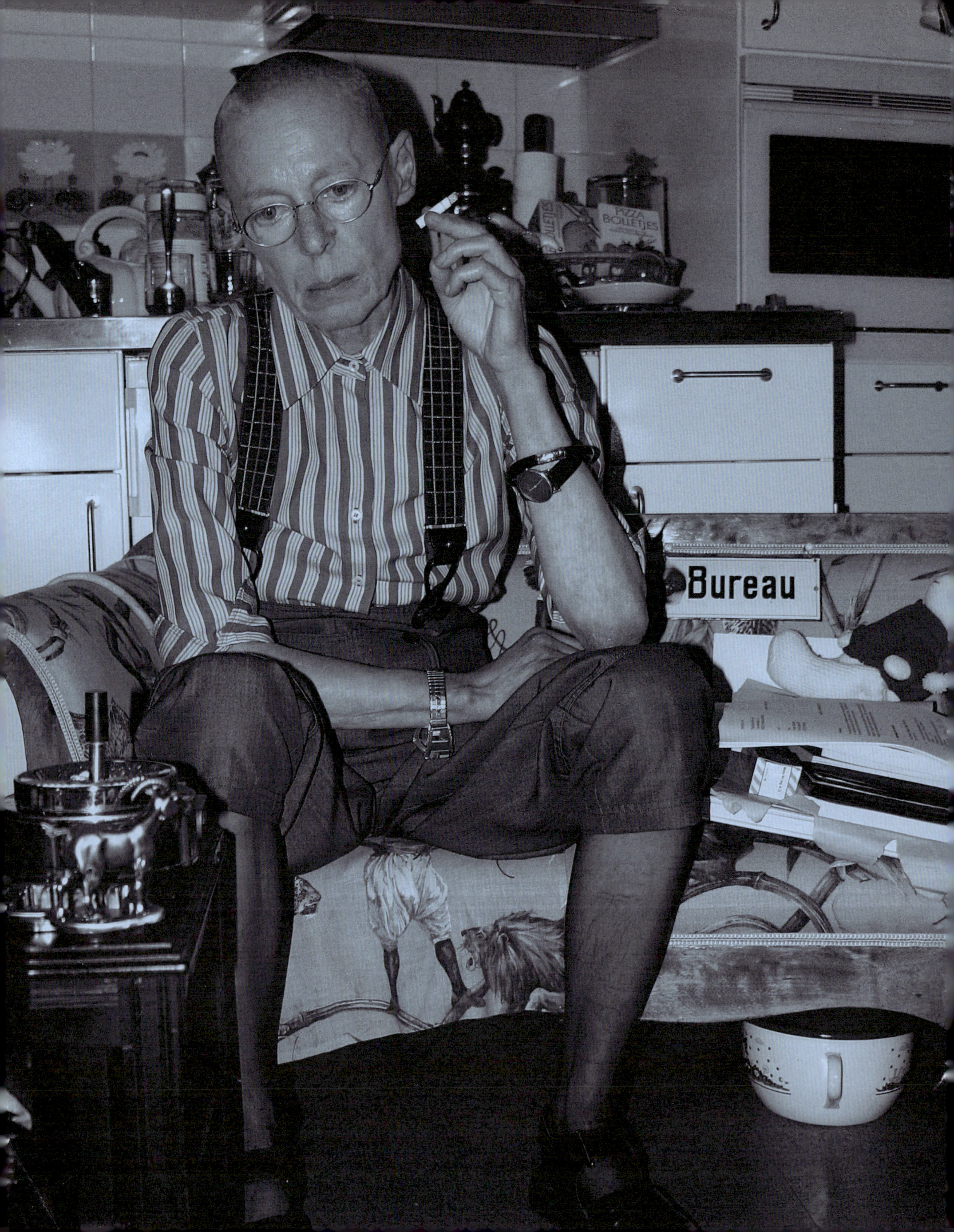
Bureau

Hanne Darboven
Hommage à Picasso

Deutsche Guggenheim

Published on the occasion of the exhibition
Hanne Darboven: Hommage à Picasso

Organized by Valerie L. Hillings

Deutsche Guggenheim, Berlin
February 4–April 23, 2006

ISBN 0-89207-341-1

Deutsche Bank & Solomon R. Guggenheim Foundation

Guggenheim Museum Publications
1071 Fifth Avenue
New York, New York 10128

Deutsche Guggenheim
Unter den Linden 13–15, 10117 Berlin

English edition available through
D.A.P./Distributed Art Publishers
155 Sixth Avenue, 2nd floor
New York, New York 10013
Tel: (212) 627-1999; Fax: (212) 627-9484

Distributed outside the United States and Canada by
Thames & Hudson, Ltd., London

Design: Eileen Boxer / BoxerDesign
Production: Cynthia Williamson
Editorial: David Grosz, Stephen Hoban

Printed in Germany by Cantz

Cover: Hanne Darboven, 2002
Frontispiece: Hanne Darboven, 2004

Photo credits:
Cover: Angelika Platen; Frontispiece, 57, 61: Svenja
Gräfin von Reichenbach; 15, 17, 19, 21, 23, 25, 27, 29, 31,
33, 35, 37, 39, 49, 51, 53, 55, 63–68, 75–80, 83, 85, 87:
Mathias Schormann; 41: Bernhard Berz; 42 (both), 44,
45, 59: Valerie L. Hillings; 46: Courtesy Elisabeth
Kaufmann, Zurich; 58: Burkhard von Harder; 81, 82:
Deutsche Guggenheim.

Copyright notices:
49: Bust of Picasso © Inge Polynice; 51: Goat ©
Wolfgang Binding; 53: Twelve signs of the zodiac, by
Meta Morfosi, published by ars mundi, Hannover.

Contents

Deutsche Guggenheim ◪

Deutsche Guggenheim is a unique joint venture between a corporation—Deutsche Bank—and a nonprofit arts foundation—The Solomon R. Guggenheim Foundation. Designed by American architect Richard Gluckman, the 510-square-meter gallery is located on the ground floor of the Deutsche Bank headquarters in Berlin. Since opening in fall 1997, Deutsche Guggenheim has presented three or four important exhibitions each year, many of which showcase a specially commissioned work by an artist. The exhibition program and day-to-day management of the museum is the responsibility of the two partners.

Deutsche Guggenheim joins the Solomon R. Guggenheim Foundation's other existing locations: the Solomon R. Guggenheim Museum in New York; the Peggy Guggenheim Collection in Venice; the Guggenheim Museum Bilbao; and the Guggenheim Hermitage in Las Vegas. Deutsche Bank regularly supports exhibitions in renowned museums, and since 1979 has been building its own collection of contemporary art under the motto "art at the workplace." The Deutsche Guggenheim initiative further represents a milestone in Deutsche Bank's advancement of the arts.

Exhibitions at Deutsche Guggenheim since its founding in 1997:

1997
Visions of Paris: Robert Delaunay's Series

1998
*James Rosenquist: The Swimmer in the Econo-Mist**

From Dürer to Rauschenberg: A Quintessence of Drawing. Masterworks from the Albertina and the Guggenheim

Katharina Sieverding: Works on Pigment

After Mountains and Sea: Frankenthaler 1956–1959

1999
*Andreas Slominski**

Georg Baselitz—Nostalgia in Istanbul

Amazons of the Avant-Garde: Alexandra Exter, Natalia Goncharova, Liubov Popova, Olga Rozanova, Varvara Stepanova, and Nadezhda Udaltsova

Dan Flavin: The Architecture of Light

2000
*Sugimoto: Portraits**

Förg—Deutsche Bank Collection

*Lawrence Weiner: Nach Alles/After All**

*Jeff Koons: Easyfun-Ethereal**

2001
The Sultan's Signature: Ottoman Calligraphy from the Sakip Sabanci Museum, Sabanci University, Istanbul

Neo Rauch—Deutsche Bank Collection

On the Sublime: Mark Rothko, Yves Klein, and James Turrell

*Rachel Whiteread: Transient Spaces**

2002
*Bill Viola: Going Forth By Day**

Kara Walker—Deutsche Bank Collection

Chillida/Tàpies

*Gerhard Richter: Eight Gray**

2003
Kazimir Malevich: Suprematism

Richard Artschwager: Up and Down/Back and Forth

Tom Sachs: Nutsy's

Bruce Nauman: Theater of Experience

2004
Miwa Yanagi—Deutsche Bank Collection

Nam June Paik: Global Groove 2004

Robert Mapplethorpe and the Classical Tradition: Photographs and Mannerist Prints

*John Baldessari: Somewhere Between Almost Right and Not Quite (With Orange)**

2005
No Limits, Just Edges: Jackson Pollock Paintings on Paper

25 Years of the Deutsche Bank Collection

Douglas Gordon's The VANITY of Allegory

*William Kentridge: Black Box/Chambre Noire**

2006
*Hanne Darboven: Hommage à Picasso**

*Commissioned work by Deutsche Guggenheim

Foreword
Dr. Tessen von Heydebreck
Member of the Board of Managing
Directors of Deutsche Bank AG

"Aquarels of German Romanticism": This was the title of one of Deutsche Bank's first Art Calendars, rediscoverable—page by page, month for month—in the collages of Hanne Darboven's installation *Kulturgeschichte 1880–1983* (*Cultural History 1880–1983*) in the Dia:Beacon Museum on the Hudson River in New York. The transformation of day-to-day life into numbers and drawn form, the connection between living and art—hardly another German artist's work displays such diverse references to Deutsche Bank's "Art in the Workplace" than Hanne Darboven's. And yet especially her reduced, plain *Schreibarbeiten* to decorate the bank's twin towers in 1986 were initially met with misunderstanding. Never having conformed, the artist has consistently and resolutely pursued her own artistic convictions, even in today's transition from drawing to applying herself to music.

Hommage à Picasso: With this series comprising nearly 10,000 sheets, we are presenting a major piece of work by Hanne Darboven in the Deutsche Guggenheim—one that reflects not just time and history, but also art itself, exemplified by one of its most important representatives. Especially conceived in close cooperation with the artist for the Deutsche Guggenheim, this exhibition is combined with the premier of Opus 60 for 120 voices, derived from the work to accompany the show acoustically.

Hanne Darboven and New York: Another connection that gives the exhibition a special background. This is the city where she developed her principal artistic ideas; here is where she created the first sketches for the "Gregorian calender," which she has made available as a model for the Limited Edition. Until today, this city has meant to the artist both fascination and the greatest possible opposite of the rural idyll in Hamburg-Harburg.

Hanne Darboven in the Deutsche Guggenheim: An idea having traveled a great distance and a long time—which has now reached its destination in Berlin, and taken on visual and musical form.

Hanne Darboven is a chronicler of history. In her work, she counts out days, months, years, and centuries in her characteristic numeric writing, and she maps the passage of time in installations that combine her signature notations with objects and images that support the overall theme of the specific work in question. She also produces music, which is adapted from her original scores in collaboration with musicologists and musicians and is based on her signature systematic modus operandi. Darboven's *Hommage à Picasso*, the Deutsche Guggenheim's eleventh commission from a contemporary artist, combines all of these aspects of her work into one installation that addresses fundamental questions about the nature of twentieth-century art—manifest in the persona and art of Pablo Picasso—and about the future of art in the twenty-first century. Both personal and universal, this remarkable installation interrogates the intersection of art and history.

The relationship between Darboven and the Guggenheim has its own history. In 1971, she was the only German artist represented in the *Guggenheim International Exhibition.* Then a mere thirty years old, Darboven had already established a place in the vanguard of Conceptual art. Thirty-five years have passed since her appearance in that show and nearly fifteen since the Solomon R. Guggenheim Museum had the great fortune to acquire a number of her works on paper from the early 1970s in the Panza Collection. Today Darboven is indisputably one of the most important living German artists and a central figure in the history of postwar art. Deutsche Guggenheim is therefore doubly pleased to add Darboven's multilayered, thought-provoking installation to the collection.

I would like to extend my sincerest gratitude to Dr. Tessen von Heydebreck, Member of the Board of Managing Directors of Deutsche Bank, who has been instrumental in recognizing the significance of the commissioning program and maintaining Deutsche Bank's significant support of the visual arts. Additional thanks are due to Dr. Ariane Grigoteit and Friedhelm Hütte, Deutsche Bank's Curators, for their continued support of the program. Hütte in particular must be acknowledged for his personal and unflagging dedication to this project from its inception. The Deutsche Guggenheim Gallery Manager Svenja Gräfin von Reichenbach is to be commended for her expert and enthusiastic oversight of the Deutsche Guggenheim's exhibition program, with the key support of Sara Bernshausen, Associate Gallery Manager. Thanks are also due to Silvie Buschmann and Lutz Driever for their help throughout the planning stages of this commission. Jörg Klambt, MuseumShop Manager, expertly shepherded the Darboven special edition through production to its elegant completion. Uwe Rommel and his team managed the construction and installation in Berlin. Nikoline Kästner, Conservator, Fabienne Lindner, Graphic Designer, Kathrin Conrad, Ulrike Heine, Daniela Mewes, and Julia Rosenbaum have each contributed to the realization of the project.

At the Solomon R. Guggenheim Museum in New York I want to acknowledge and thank the exhibition's curator, Dr. Valerie L. Hillings, Curatorial Assistant, for organizing this exhibition and commission. I would also like to recognize with gratitude Lisa Dennison, Director of the Solomon R. Guggenheim Museum and Chief Curator; Nancy Spector, Curator of Contemporary Art; Jill Kohler, Associate Registrar for Collection Management; Maria Pallante-Hyun, Associate General Counsel & Director of Licensing; Gabrielle Decamous, 2005–06 Hilla Rebay Fellow; and Alison Weaver, Director of Program Management, Affiliates.

This catalogue was made possible by the Guggenheim's outstanding Publications department, in particular Elizabeth Levy, Director of Publications; Elizabeth Franzen, Managing Editor; David Grosz, Associate Editor; Stephen Hoban, Assistant Managing Editor; and Cynthia Williamson, Associate Production Manager. It has been a pleasure to work once again with catalogue designer Eileen Boxer. As usual, her work simultaneously takes into account the formal qualities of the artist's signature style and expresses her own innovative vision for the book.

I would like to express my appreciation to the authors of this book, Anne Rorimer, Valerie L. Hillings, Wolfgang Marx, Gerd de Vries, Sybille Omlin, and Svenja Gräfin von Reichenbach. All of their contributions illuminate key aspects of Darboven's art and in doing so, they demonstrate how this commission fits into the artist's larger body of work.

Finally, I would like to thank Paul Maenz and Gerd de Vries for their role in facilitating the commission and various aspects of the project as a whole.

Anne Rorimer

Toward the development of the means to embody a tangible, yet nonmaterial, transcription of temporal and spatial relationships, Hanne Darboven began in the late 1960s to investigate the myriad permutations provided by the four to six digits needed to notate the day, month, and year of a standard Gregorian calendar date. Her numerical sequences, differently conceived for each work, are based on the dates that exist within the span of an entire century—without, however, including the first two numbers of the year (i.e., the 1 and the 9 of the twentieth century). Thus 1 January 1969 is represented as 1,1,69, and these numbers (1, 1, 6, 9) become the basis for various calculations and permutations, an example of which is indicated in the following excerpt from Darboven's catalogue pages for the exhibition *Konzeption/Conception*, held at the Städtisches Museum, Leverkusen, in 1969:

CALCULATION EXAMPLE:
1.1.69 = 1 + 1 + 6 + 9 = 17 $\rightarrow$ 1X = No 1 = 17K
2.1.69 = 2 + 1 + 6 + 9 = 18} $\rightarrow$ 2X = No 2 = 18K
1.2.69 = 1 + 2 + 6 + 9 = 18}

THE DIGITS 6 AND 9 ARE CALCULATED SEPARATELY. ALL OTHER DOUBLE-DIGIT NUMBERS ARE CALCULATED AS A UNIT. ALL NOTATIONS ARE RECORDED IN NUMBERS. EACH NUMBER IS REPEATED AS MANY TIMES AS THE FACE VALUE INDICATES.

SAMPLE:
1.1.69 = 1 × 1 / 1 × 1 / 6 × 6 / 9 × 9 /
31.12.69 = 31 × 31 / 12 × 12 / 6 × 6 / 9 × 9 /[2]

In the Leverkusen catalogue, numbers designating dates add up to 17, at their lowest sum, and accumulate through 58 (i.e., 31 + 12 + 6 + 9) at their highest and serve to define each successive tally over the space of four pages.

Numbers in any one work by Darboven may be typed and/or handwritten either as Arabic or Roman numerals or may be expressed as verbal symbols in either German or English. Her numerical systems, unwinding on paper, ensure an endless variety of permutations. "Many variations exist in my work," she states. "There is constant flexibility and changeability, evidencing the relentless flux of events."[3] The resulting "figurative" imagery of her computations attests to the almost ceaseless stream of mental energy that accounts for the great range of visual diversity originating with the artist's tabulations and delineations, notations and underscorings, diagrams, charts, and cross-outs.

Darboven's intricate arithmetic procedures and permutations yield visual and thematic testimony to the idea that making art entails total immersion and steadfast attention. Her oeuvre represents, in and of itself, a lifetime commitment to the mental and physical demands of aesthetic activity and the understanding that such a commitment must be carried out within the framework of ongoing and passing time. In 1968, having completed her formal art studies in Hamburg, Germany, and living in New York since 1966, she devised the principle that underlies the majority of her works.[4] Her realization that calendar dates might supply endless computational possibilities resulting from addition and multiplication provided her with a guiding structure on the one hand and an open-ended, unconfined freedom for action on the other. They have guaranteed her an unending source of numbers that have served in countless combinations.

Whether intimate in scale, filling an entire exhibition space, or taking the form of a book, Darboven's works are striking in view of the numerous calculations whose intricacies are plotted in advance and laid out in what the artist refers to as the "Index." The numerical formulas from which a particular work is spawned may leave the viewer "spellbound by the magic."[5] Inasmuch as the underlying scheme of each work, however inherently straightforward and basic, manifests a high degree of complexity. Darboven maintained in 1968 that "I could not restructure any of my systems by starting them methodically from their respective beginnings. For these depend on work previously done."[6] She has stated furthermore that "the plan can only provide an impulse,"[7] which originates at its most fundamental level with 2 = 1, 2; 1 + 1 = 1, 2, etc. (which she uses on her personal ink stamp almost like a logo to signify the principle of her system).

Much preliminary thought precedes the writing out of each of Darboven's works from start to finish, and the artist thus emphasizes the importance of the plan as a starting point more than as an end in itself "I investigate my formulas which I build myself, almost to the point of saturation with knowledge—and then I do them."[8] By means of her temporally based formulas Darboven liberates numbers from their quantifying function to imbue them with a graphic function instead. "I only use numbers because it is a way of writing without describing [*Schreiben nicht beschreiben*],"[9] she has stressed and further insists that her work "has nothing to do with mathematics. Nothing! . . . A number of something (two chairs, or whatever) is something else. It's not pure number and has other meanings."[10]

The sum of Darboven's diagrams and notations takes over from traditional compositional elements of shape and form to represent the passage of time through passages of written numbers and words that do not refer to anything but themselves. As Coosje van Bruggen has encapsulated it, "the changing dates are a record and a reminder of time passing. Irrevocably, tomorrow will turn into today or [in German] 'heute,' which Darboven will write as a word on the page only to cross it out, signifying time spent."[11] The crossed-out "heute" further suggests, as on a list of things to do, that yet another day of work has been accomplished. The meaning of such passages lies in their self-reflexive, denotative nature. The artist has sought to remove any possible shade of meaning from her notations so that numbers and words might occupy the space of the paper or the page of a book as self-evident visual constructions.

"I use no forms of expression,"[12] Darboven has emphasized. At the core of her oeuvre is the premise that the time put into a work is its own overarching message. Darboven's art is founded on her dedication to the magnitude of her endeavor and the "realization" that art results from the time bestowed on its production. "'Art' is work . . . not every work is art but art is work and vice versa," the artist has written.[13] Time, in conjunction with the mental and physical energy given to a project, and the demarcation of time as it proceeds from one day to the next— leaving an accumulation of personal and historical events behind it—are fused within Darboven's work as a unified representational totality.

Notes

1   The essay is adapted from Anne Rorimer, *New Art in the 60s and 70s: Redefining Reality* (London: Thames & Hudson, 2001), pp. 164–71. Reproduced with permission of the author.
2   *Konzeption/Conception*, exh. cat. (Leverkusen: Städtisches Museum, 1969). This translation by Horst Schastok.
3   Hanne Darboven, [Statement in] "Artists on Their Art," *Art International* 12, no. 4 (April 20, 1968), p. 55.
4   See Klaus Honnef, "Art Encyclopedias of Culture: Klaus Honnef on Hanne Darboven," in *Hanne Darboven: Primitive Zeit/Uhrzeit, Primitive Clock/Clock Time*, exh. cat. (Philadelphia: Goldie Paley Gallery, Moore College of Art and Design, 1990), p. 7. In the daily process of recording her appointments and keeping track of her activities in her diary, Darboven noticed the numerical progressions occurring with each day's change in date.
5   Johannes Cladders, text, trans. Richard Bairstow, in "Hanne Darboven: 6 Manuskripte *'69',*" *Kunst-Zeitung* 3 (July 1969).
6   Darboven, quoted in "Artists on Their Art," p. 55.
7   Darboven, quoted in Amine Haase, "An Interview with Hanne Darboven," trans. Michael Schultz, in *Hanne Darboven: Primitive Zeit/Uhrzeit*, p. 13.
8   Darboven, quoted in Ingrid Burgbacher-Krupka, "On 'the Concept of Time,' A Conversation with Hanne Darboven," in *Hanne Darboven. Konstruiert, Literarisch, Musikalisch/Constructed, Literary, Musical: The Sculpting of Time* (Ostfildern: Cantz, 1994), p. 72.
9   Darboven, quoted in Lucy R. Lippard, "Hanne Darboven: Deep in Numbers," *Artforum* 12, no. 2 (October 1973), p. 35.
10   Ibid., pp. 35–36.
11   Coosje van Bruggen, "Afterword: Today Crossed Out," in *Hanne Darboven: Primitive Zeit/Uhrzeit*, p. 3.
12   Darboven, in *Hanne Darboven: Primitive Zeit/Uhrzeit*, p. 13.
13   Hanne Darboven, letter to Sol LeWitt, October 19, 1973, Sol LeWitt Collection, Wadsworth Atheneum, Hartford.

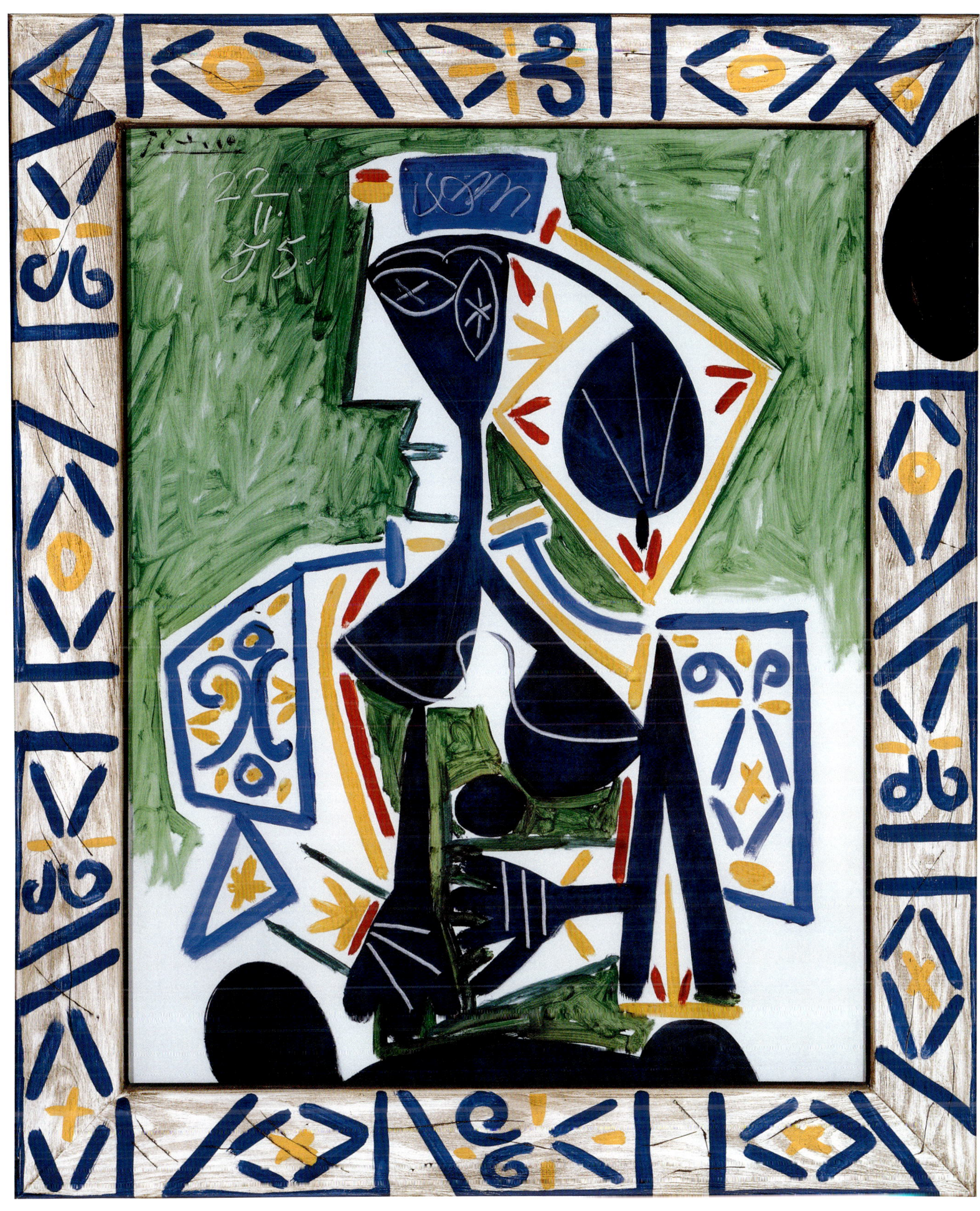

Framed reproduction of Pablo Picasso's
Seated Figure in Turkish Costume (1955;
Collection of Hamburger Kunsthalle), from
Hanne Darboven, *Hommage à Picasso*,
1995–2006. Lithograph in painted wooden
frame, 99.2 × 82.5 cm.

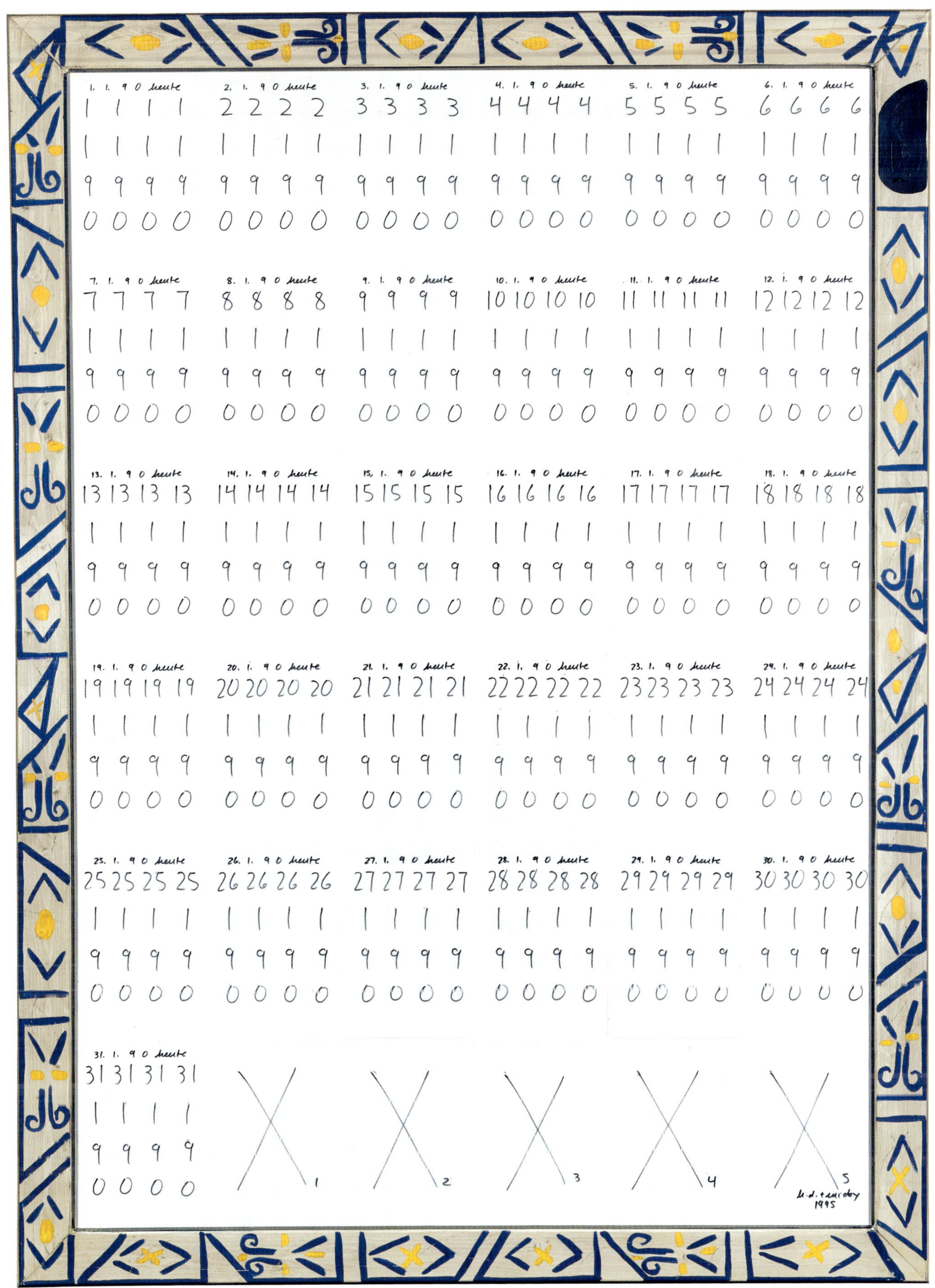

Framed text panels, from Hanne Darboven,
Hommage à Picasso, 1995–2006.
Felt-tip pen on parchment paper in painted
wooden frames, 196.5 × 144 cm each panel,
36 sheets per panel, 30 × 21 cm each sheet.

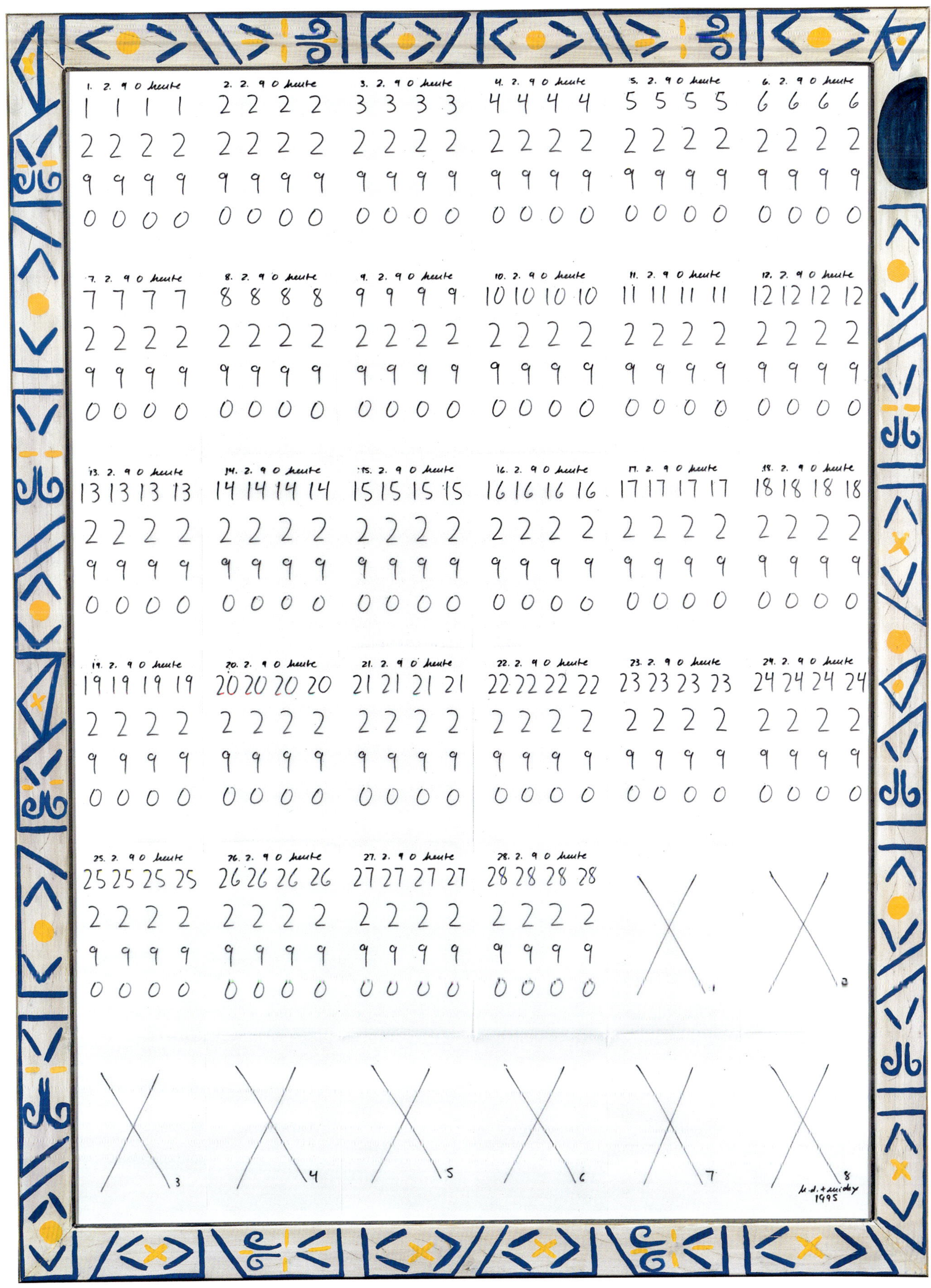

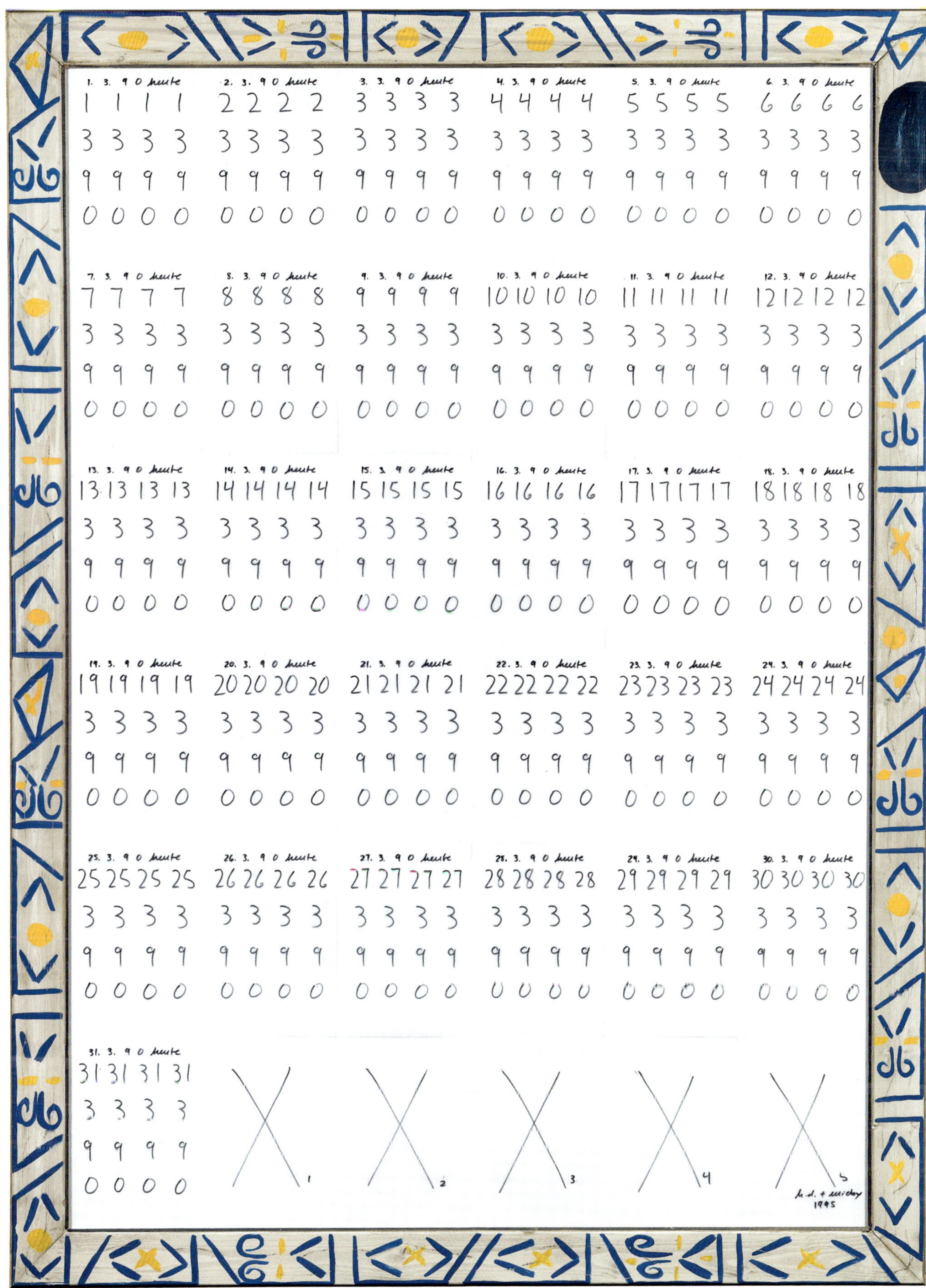

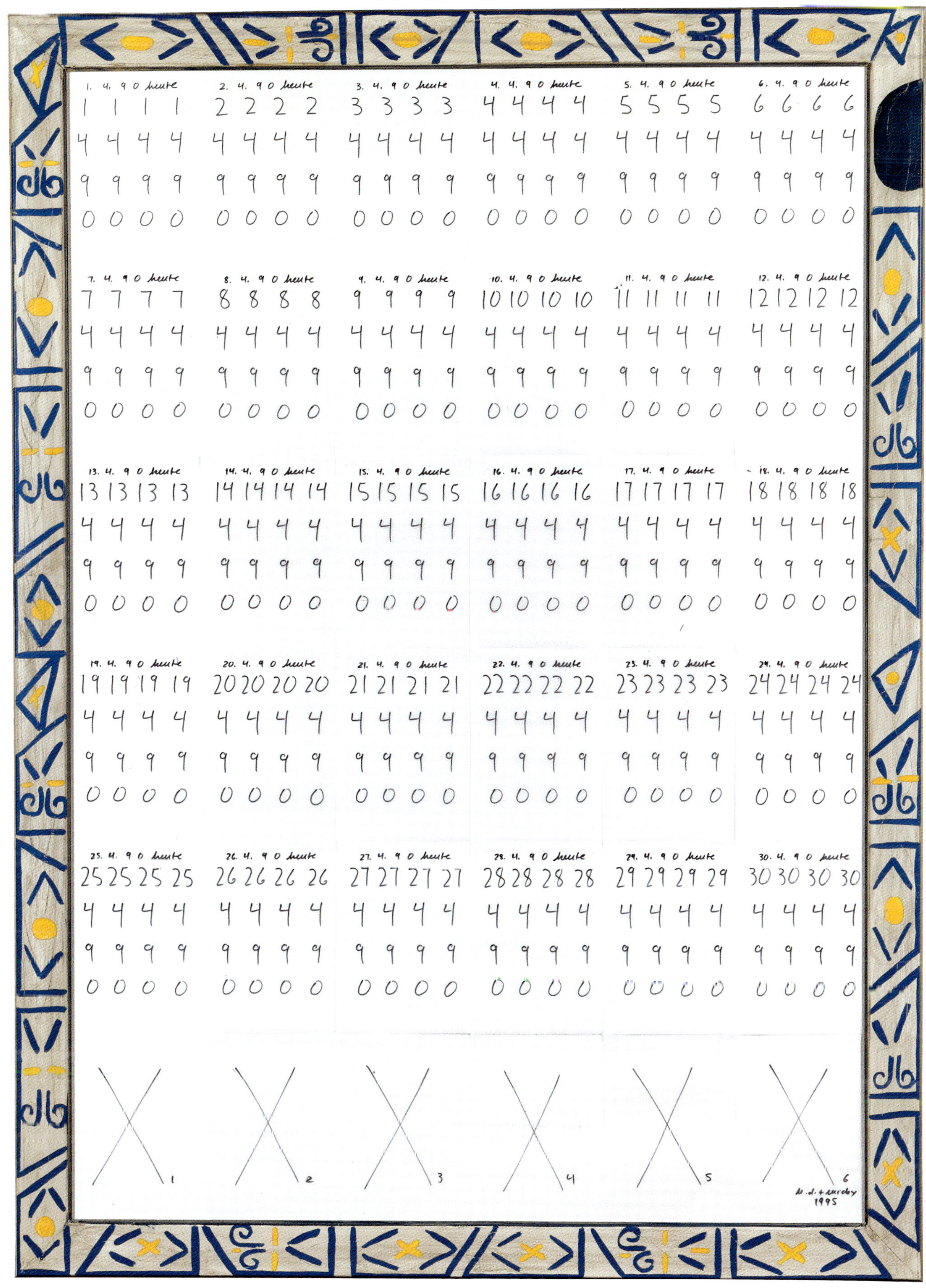

1. 4. 9 0 heute
2. 4. 9 0 heute
3. 4. 9 0 heute
4. 4. 9 0 heute
5. 4. 9 0 heute
6. 4. 9 0 heute
1 1 1 1   2 2 2 2   3 3 3 3   4 4 4 4   5 5 5 5   6 6 6 6
4 4 4 4   4 4 4 4   4 4 4 4   4 4 4 4   4 4 4 4   4 4 4 4
9 9 9 9   9 9 9 9   9 9 9 9   9 9 9 9   9 9 9 9   9 9 9 9
0 0 0 0   0 0 0 0   0 0 0 0   0 0 0 0   0 0 0 0   0 0 0 0
7. 4. 9 0 heute
8. 4. 9 0 heute
9. 4. 9 0 heute
10. 4. 9 0 heute
11. 4. 9 0 heute
12. 4. 9 0 heute
7 7 7 7   8 8 8 8   9 9 9 9   10 10 10 10   11 11 11 11   12 12 12 12
4 4 4 4   4 4 4 4   4 4 4 4   4 4 4 4   4 4 4 4   4 4 4 4
9 9 9 9   9 9 9 9   9 9 9 9   9 9 9 9   9 9 9 9   9 9 9 9
0 0 0 0   0 0 0 0   0 0 0 0   0 0 0 0   0 0 0 0   0 0 0 0
13. 4. 9 0 heute
14. 4. 9 0 heute
15. 4. 9 0 heute
16. 4. 9 0 heute
17. 4. 9 0 heute
18. 4. 9 0 heute
13 13 13 13   14 14 14 14   15 15 15 15   16 16 16 16   17 17 17 17   18 18 18 18
4 4 4 4   4 4 4 4   4 4 4 4   4 4 4 4   4 4 4 4   4 4 4 4
9 9 9 9   9 9 9 9   9 9 9 9   9 9 9 9   9 9 9 9   9 9 9 9
0 0 0 0   0 0 0 0   0 0 0 0   0 0 0 0   0 0 0 0   0 0 0 0
19. 4. 9 0 heute
20. 4. 9 0 heute
21. 4. 9 0 heute
22. 4. 9 0 heute
23. 4. 9 0 heute
24. 4. 9 0 heute
19 19 19 19   20 20 20 20   21 21 21 21   22 22 22 22   23 23 23 23   24 24 24 24
4 4 4 4   4 4 4 4   4 4 4 4   4 4 4 4   4 4 4 4   4 4 4 4
9 9 9 9   9 9 9 9   9 9 9 9   9 9 9 9   9 9 9 9   9 9 9 9
0 0 0 0   0 0 0 0   0 0 0 0   0 0 0 0   0 0 0 0   0 0 0 0
25. 4. 9 0 heute
26. 4. 9 0 heute
27. 4. 9 0 heute
28. 4. 9 0 heute
29. 4. 9 0 heute
30. 4. 9 0 heute
25 25 25 25   26 26 26 26   27 27 27 27   28 28 28 28   29 29 29 29   30 30 30 30
4 4 4 4   4 4 4 4   4 4 4 4   4 4 4 4   4 4 4 4   4 4 4 4
9 9 9 9   9 9 9 9   9 9 9 9   9 9 9 9   9 9 9 9   9 9 9 9
0 0 0 0   0 0 0 0   0 0 0 0   0 0 0 0   0 0 0 0   0 0 0 0
1   2   3   4   5   6
1995

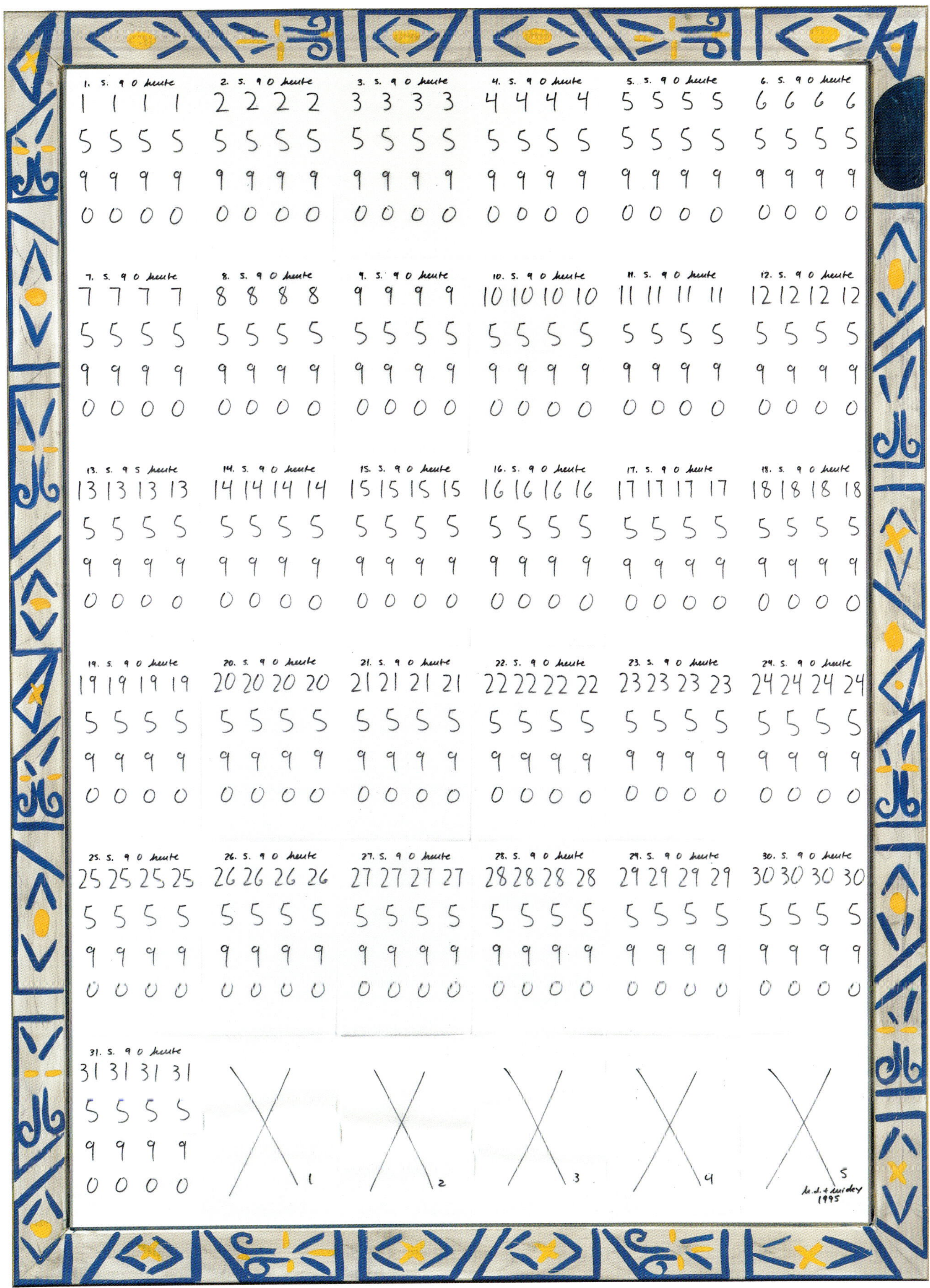

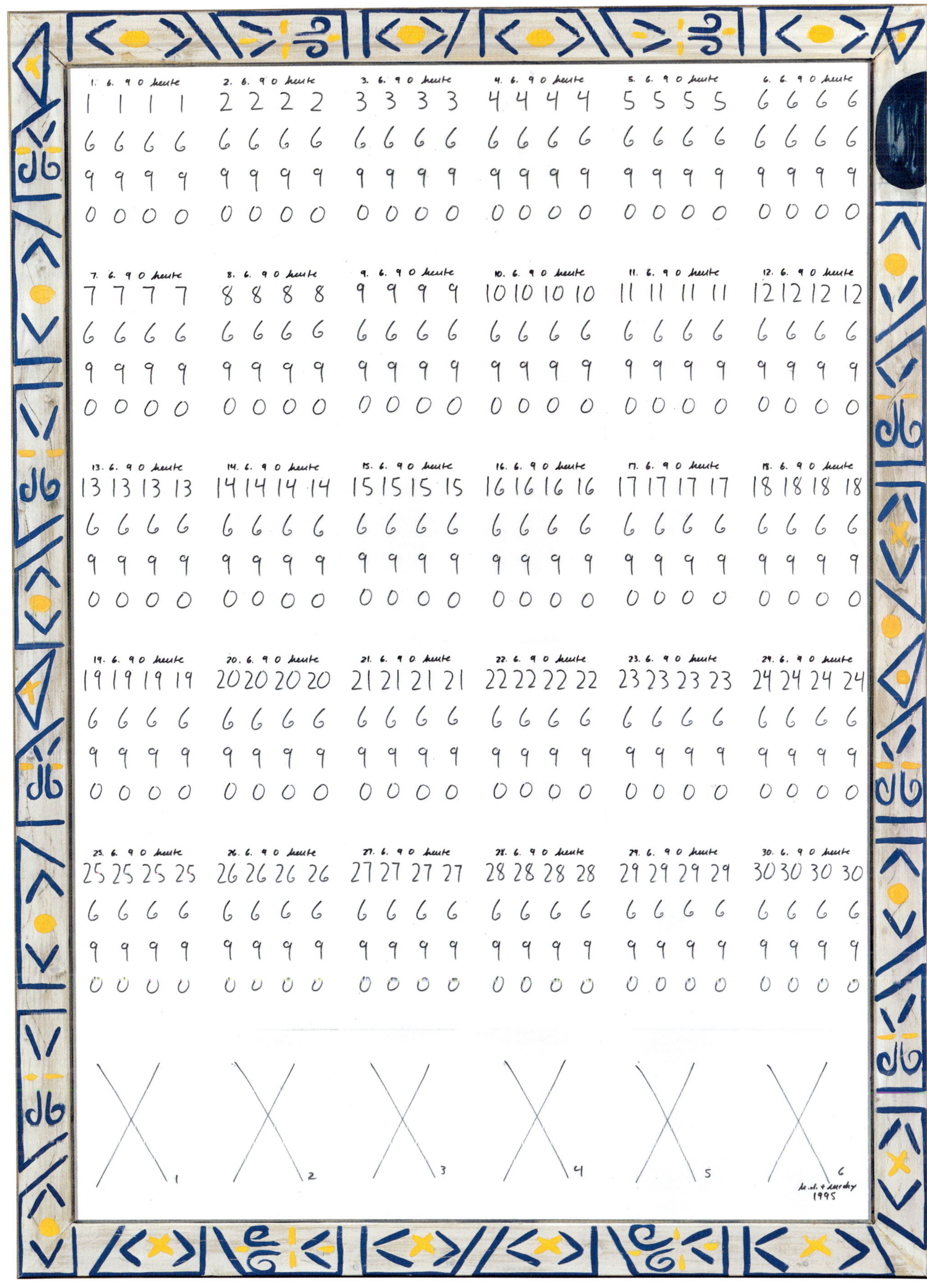

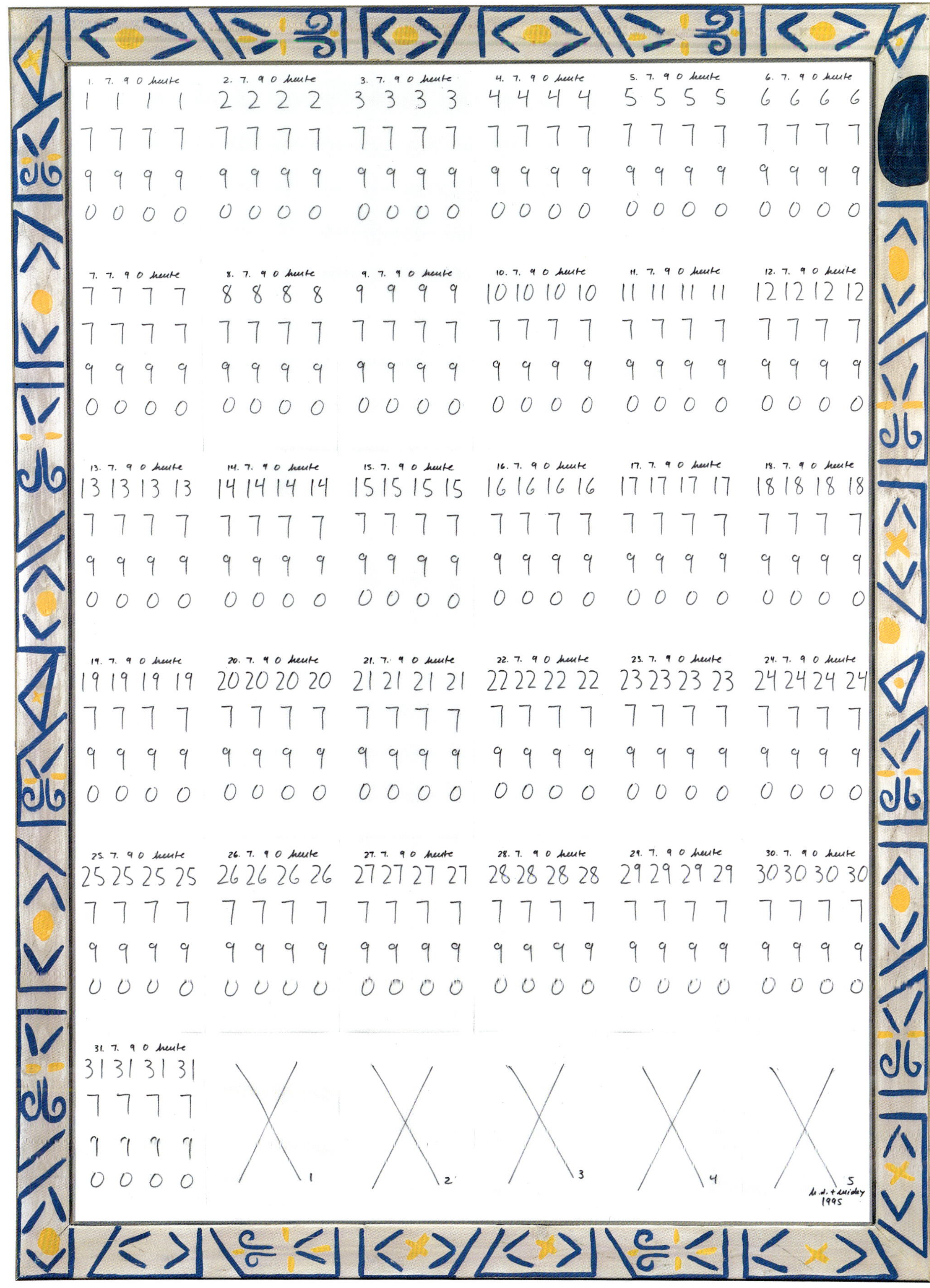

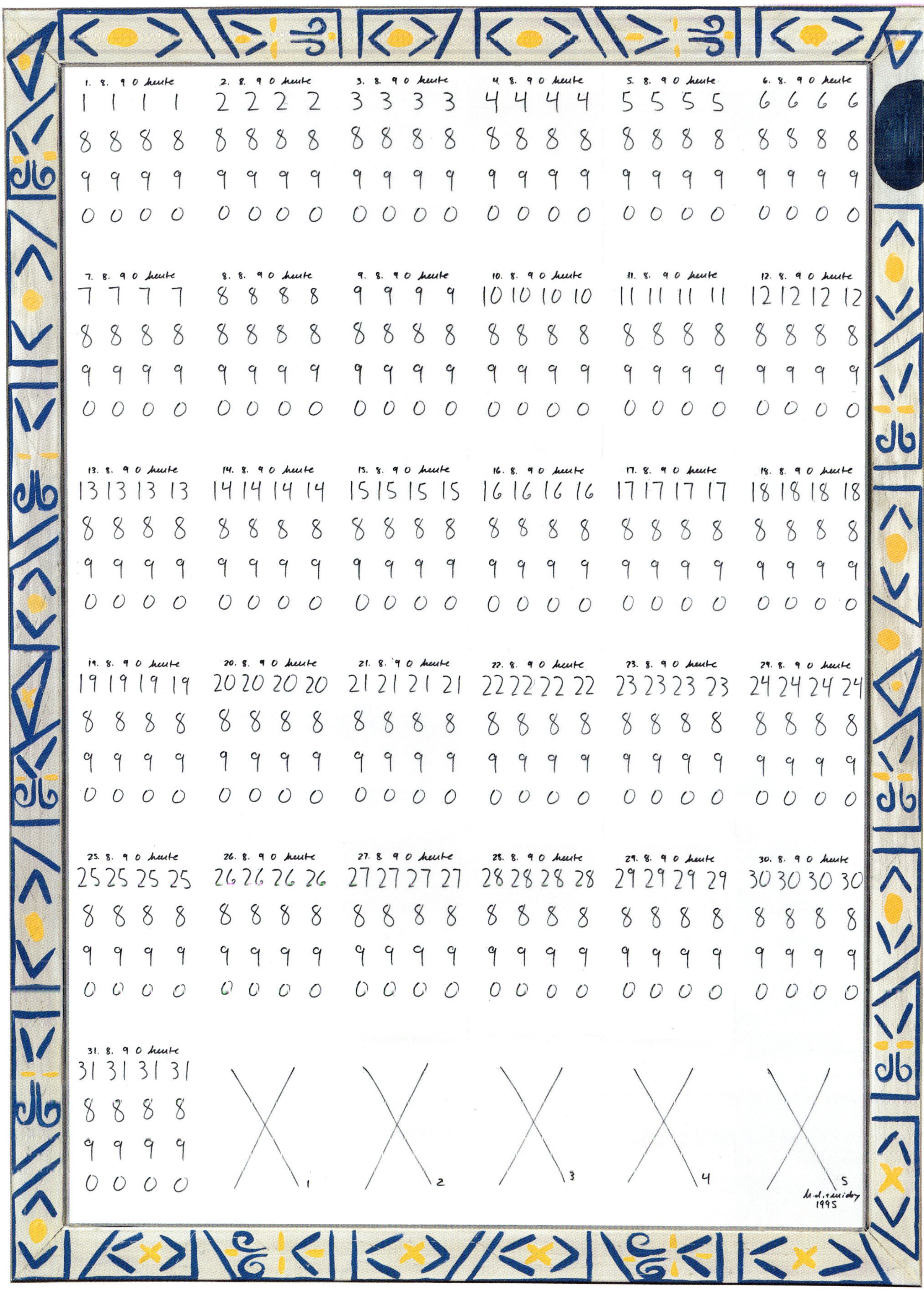

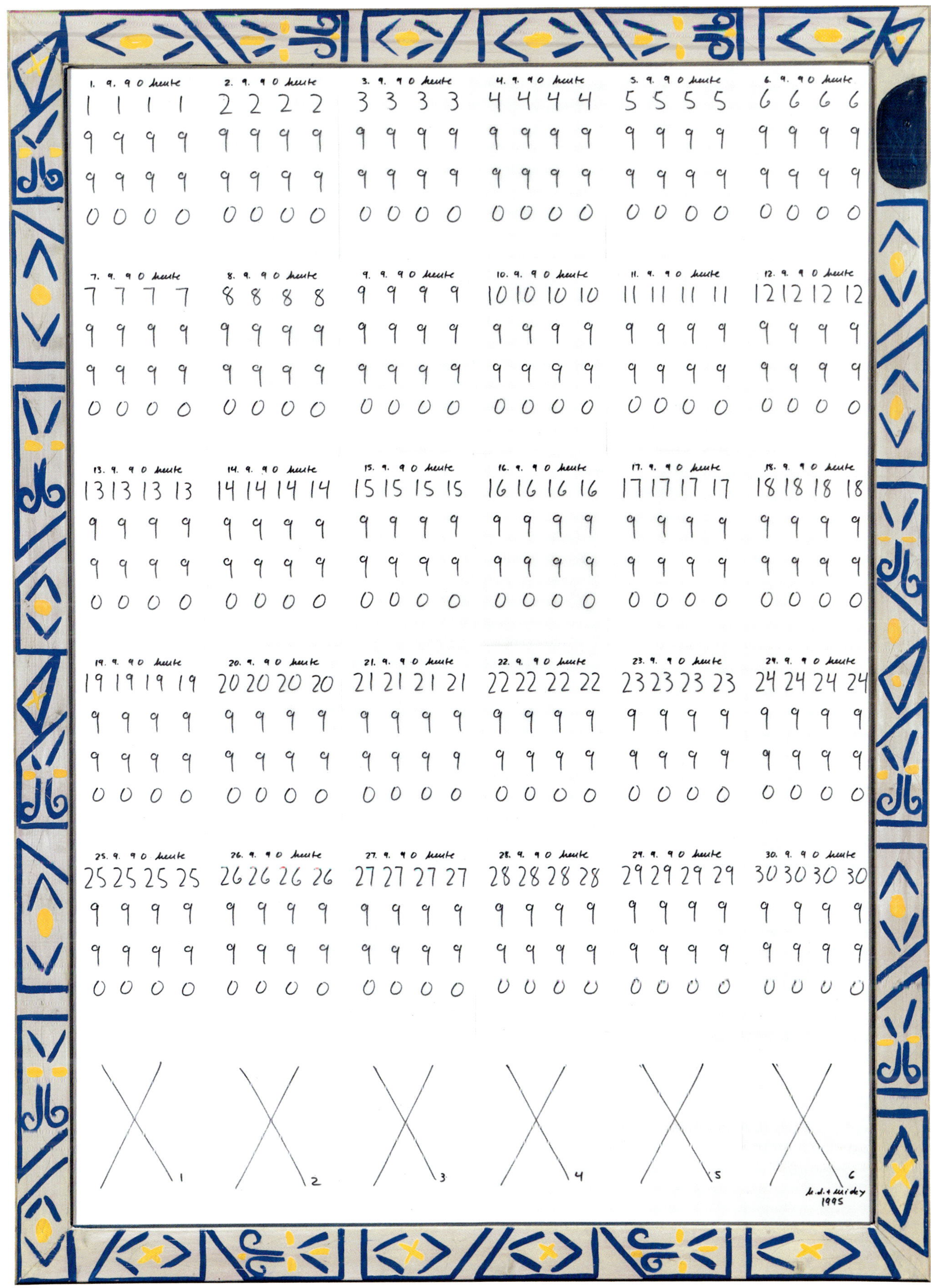

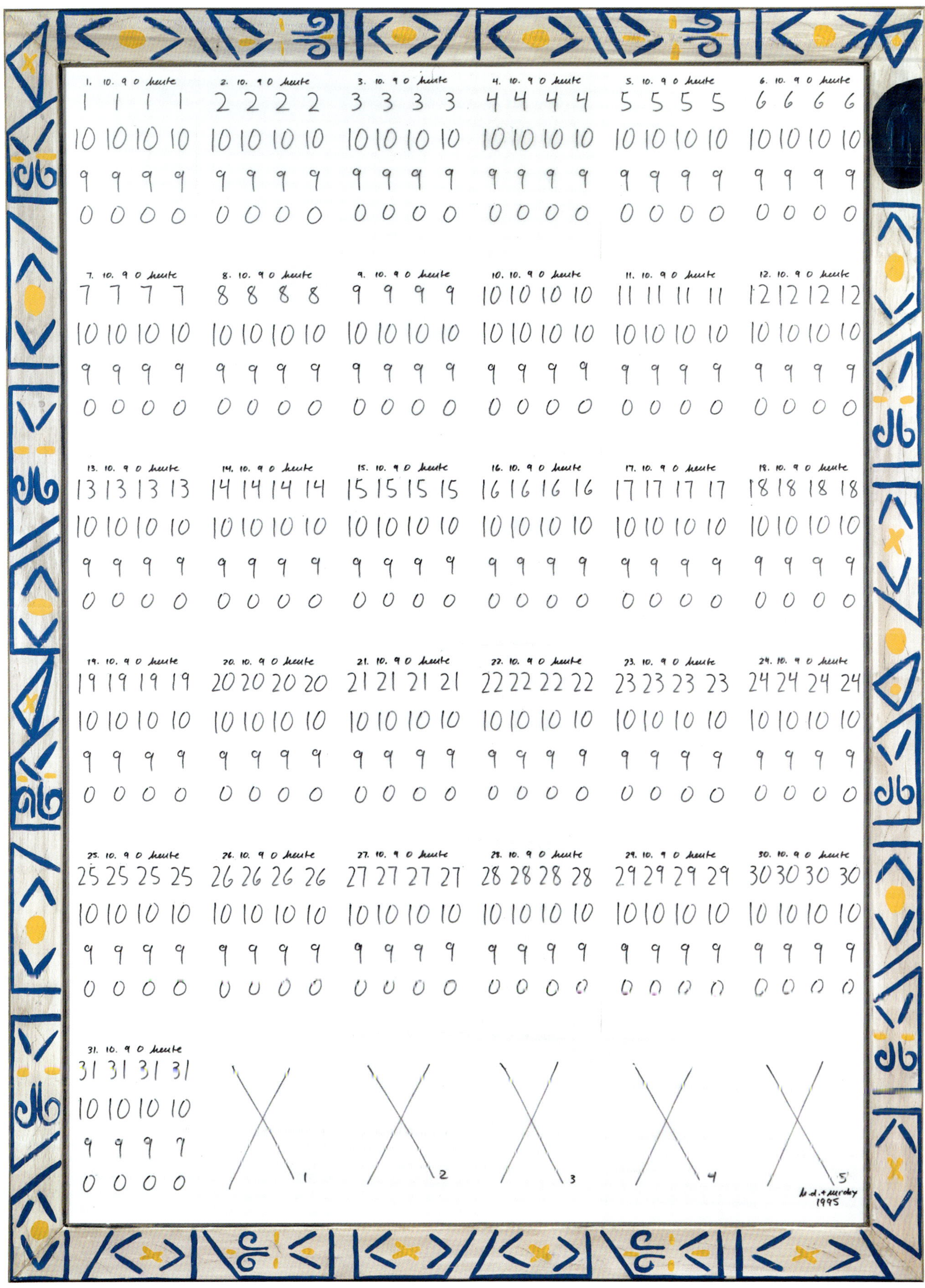

1. 10. 9 0 heute   2. 10. 9 0 heute   3. 10. 9 0 heute   4. 10. 9 0 heute   5. 10. 9 0 heute   6. 10. 9 0 heute
7. 10. 9 0 heute   8. 10. 9 0 heute   9. 10. 9 0 heute   10. 10. 9 0 heute   11. 10. 9 0 heute   12. 10. 9 0 heute
13. 10. 9 0 heute   14. 10. 9 0 heute   15. 10. 9 0 heute   16. 10. 9 0 heute   17. 10. 9 0 heute   18. 10. 9 0 heute
19. 10. 9 0 heute   20. 10. 9 0 heute   21. 10. 9 0 heute   22. 10. 9 0 heute   23. 10. 9 0 heute   24. 10. 9 0 heute
25. 10. 9 0 heute   26. 10. 9 0 heute   27. 10. 9 0 heute   28. 10. 9 0 heute   29. 10. 9 0 heute   30. 10. 9 0 heute
31. 10. 9 0 heute
1
2
3
4
5
1995

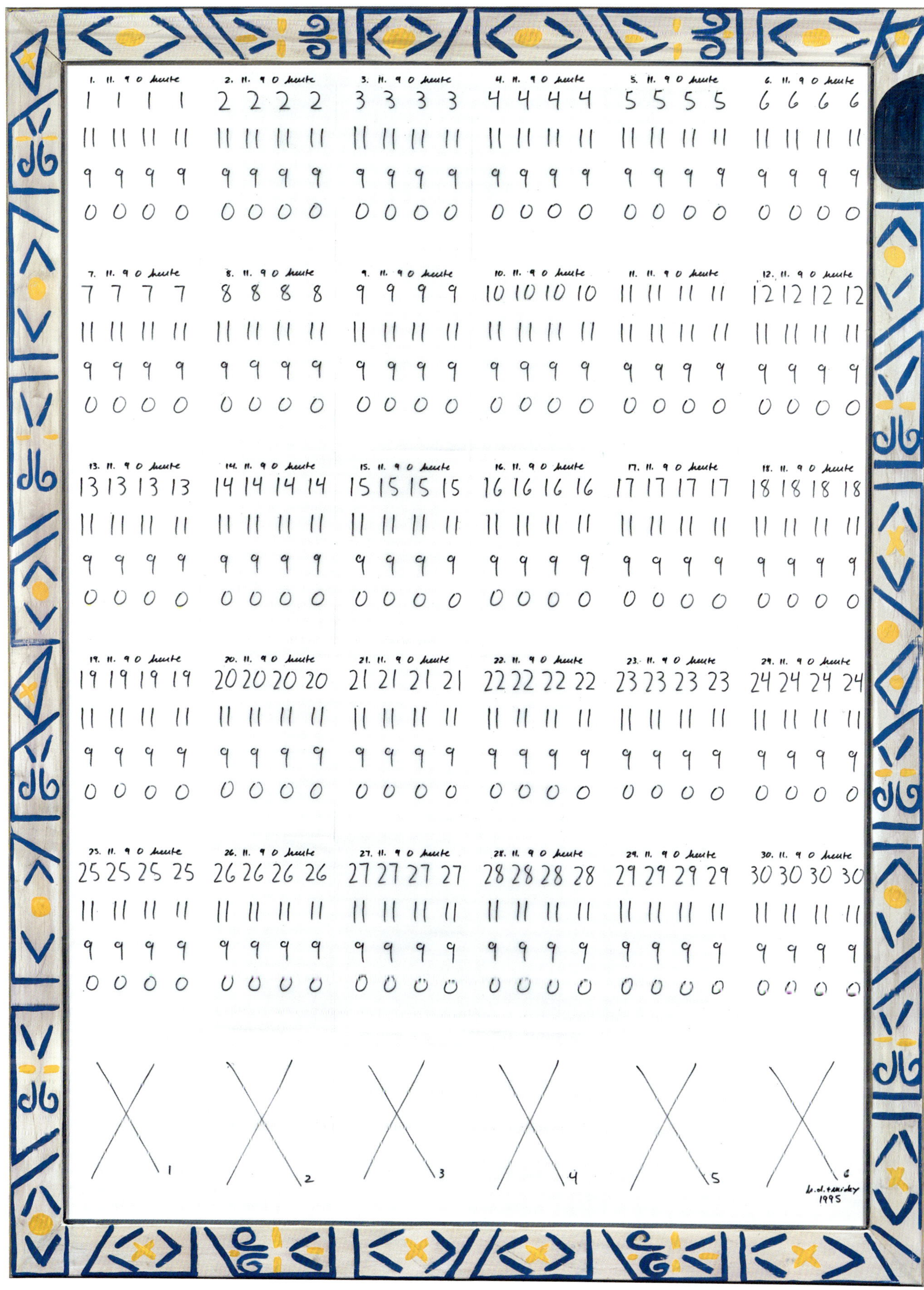

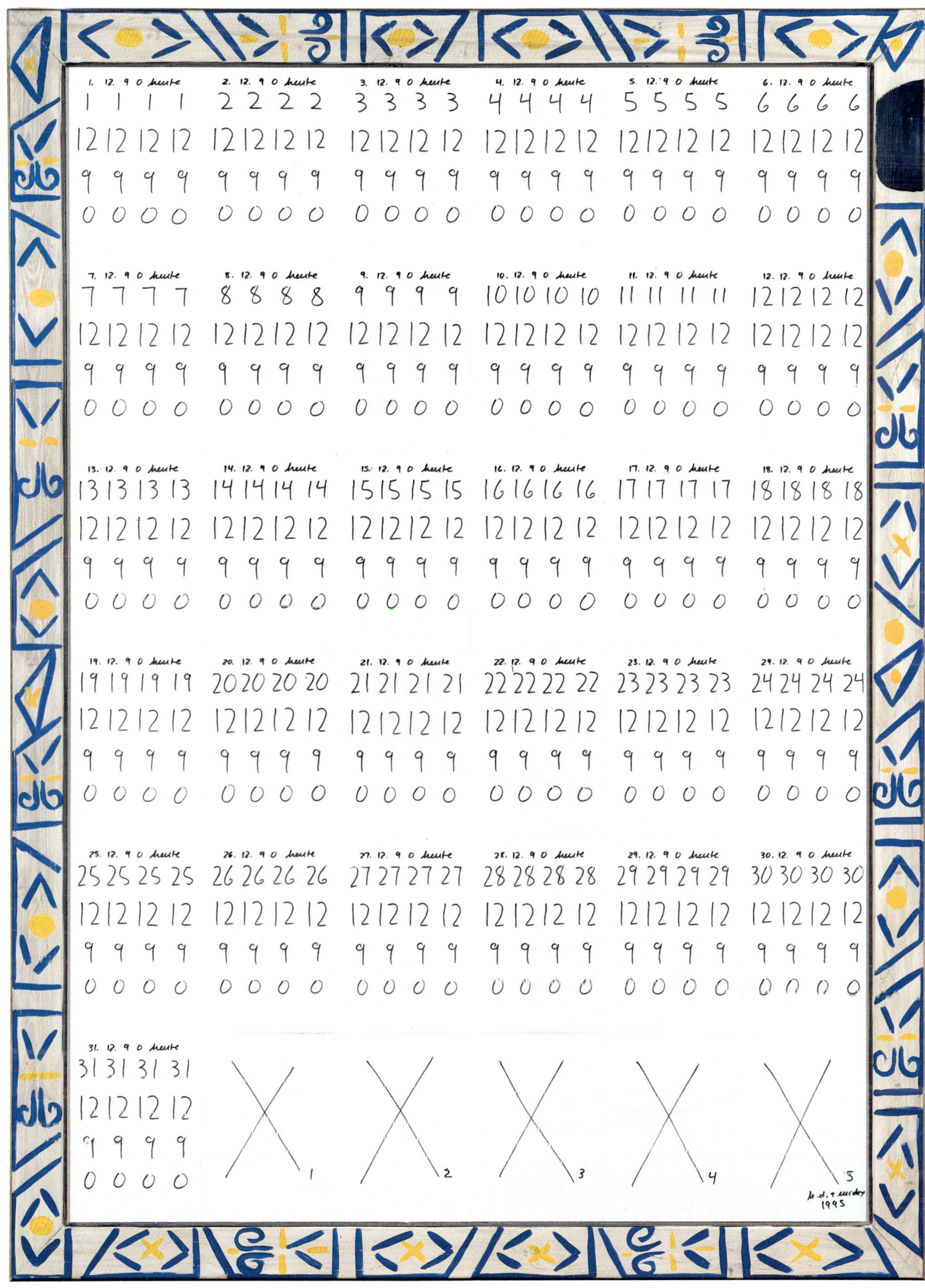

A Portrait of the Artists: Hanne Darboven's *Hommage à Picasso*

Valerie L. Hillings

Upon entering Hanne Darboven's (b. 1941) home and studio, it becomes quite evident that she is not only an artist, but also an avid collector and astute curator. In every direction—up, down, left, right—one encounters an overwhelming visual cacophony that at first suggests chaos and clutter, but upon closer inspection reveals a logical order that is both formally and intellectually rich. In this sense, Darboven's home-cum-museum-cum-archive constitutes an endlessly stimulating installation that reflects and illuminates the dialectic nature of her work in its fusion of the extreme precision, even monotony, of her daily numeric writing[1] with the kitschy liveliness of such disparate cultural artifacts as a life-sized wooden horse, hand puppets, and a surrealist chair reminiscent of the art of Joan Miró. The intentional juxtaposition of objects that have been incorporated into Darboven's artworks with personal items like an oft-worn vest covered with pins and buttons or a plaque reading "Mama Micky und Klein Micky" on the door leading to her backyard—home to her beloved pet goat, Micky—simultaneously narrates cultural and personal history. Taken together, the contents of Darboven's home constitute a sort of self-portrait writ large.

Similarly, Darboven's installation *Hommage à Picasso* brings together disparate personal and cultural objects to paint a double portrait of the artists Pablo Picasso and Hanne Darboven. The piece consists of 9,720 sheets of Darboven's handwritten numeric writing, which are divided into 270 framed panels; a lithograph of Picasso's 1955 painting *Seated Figure in Turkish Costume,*[2]

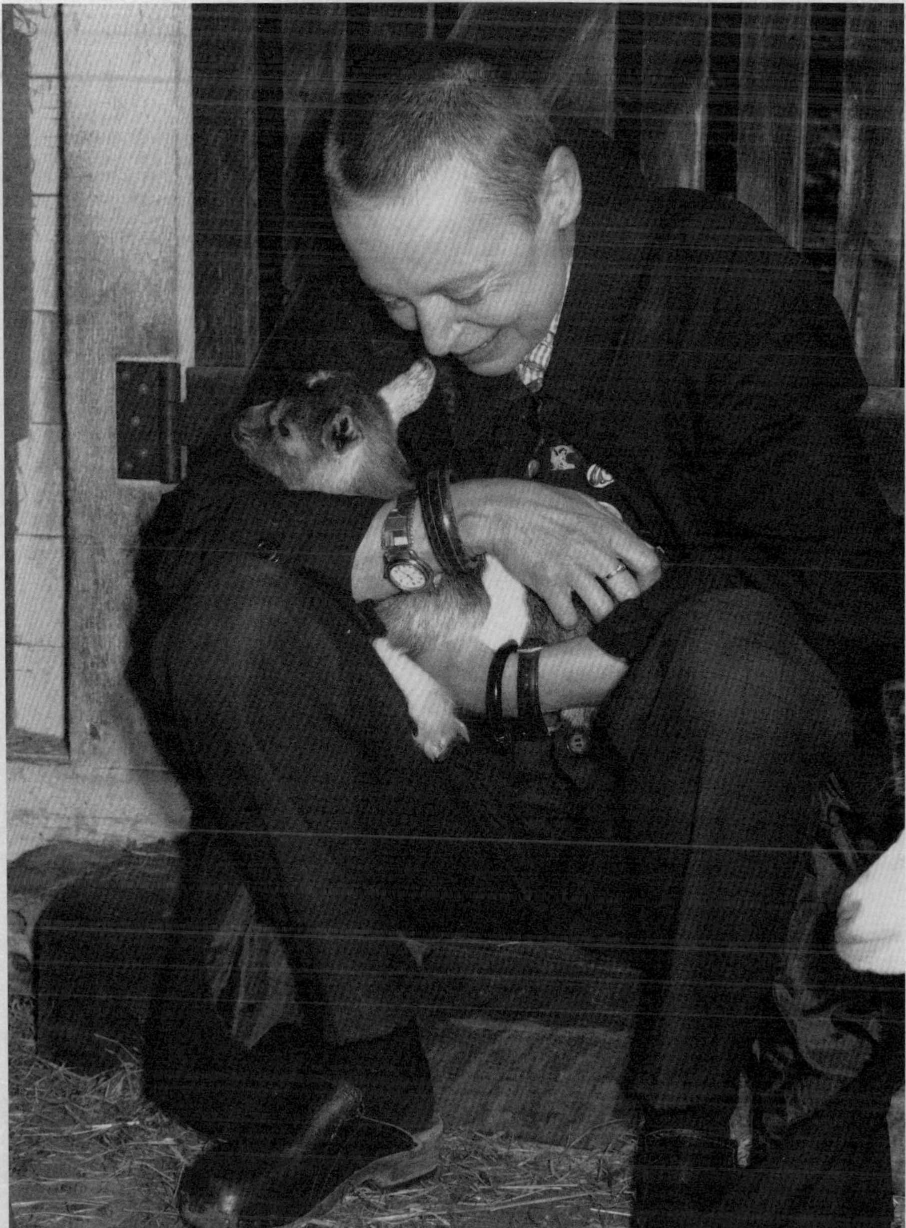

HANNE DARBOVEN AND WURTZY, CA. 2000

also framed; a series of purchased and commissioned sculptures ranging from a bronze, Roman-style bust of Picasso to three birch-twig donkeys fashioned by Polish folk artists; and an original, 120-part orchestral work, Opus 60, adapted from the artist's autograph by the musicologist Wolfgang Marx. With this multifaceted work, Darboven examines the role of repetition and citation in art. To this end, she interrogates both the concept of signature style, which is fundamentally about self-referentiality and the consistent reiteration of artistic motifs and approaches, as well as the practice of directly engaging the work of another artist, either in homage or as a means to one's own creative ends. Thus, the very notion of originality stands at the core of *Hommage à Picasso*.

POINT OF DEPARTURE

Darboven began her art studies in 1952 at age eleven, and in 1962, she enrolled at the Hochschule für bildende Künste in Hamburg. Her early student works reflect the influence of European Art Informel, a mode still au courant in the early 1960s.[3] During a visit to *documenta 3* in 1964, which was heavily dominated by artists associated with Informel and American action painting, Darboven was deeply impressed by the work of the German group Zero (Heinz Mack, Otto Piene, and Günther Uecker) and that of the Germany-based Brazilian artist Almir Mavignier. Employing serial repetition, the Cartesian grid, and sculptural relief as central aspects of their work, these artists and others of their generation were producing work that straddled definitions of painting and sculpture.

Darboven learned about these approaches firsthand when she studied with Mavignier during his first term as a professor at the Hochschule in Hamburg in 1965. The Brazilian imparted to his students the lessons of his distinguished teachers at the Hochschule für Gestaltung in Ulm, who included the Swiss artist Max Bill, a pioneer of Concrete art and advocate of a mathematical approach to art; Josef Albers, the great color theorist of the Bauhaus; and Max Bense, a leading figure in the emerging field of information theory. From these influences, Mavignier had devised an objective system for art that entailed using a large nail to apply vividly colored, thick dots of paint to the canvas to produce a series of geometric forms—most commonly squares. Following his example, Darboven was soon producing monochrome paintings that took the grid as their organizing principle and contained geometric reliefs fashioned from materials ranging from paint to nails.

By 1966 Darboven had left both the Hochschule and Germany and moved to New York. But Mavignier's conceptual lessons clearly left an imprint on the young artist, as she developed her own systematic, abstract method. Employing the neutral language of numbers and pen, pencil, the typewriter, and graph paper as materials, she began to make simple linear constructions of numbers called *Konstruktionen*. In these early pieces, the graph paper's grid structure seems almost to shape the work, as can be seen in the artist's frequent use of square forms and 4 x 4 groupings of numbers, both handwritten and typed. It was these *Konstruktionen* that garnered the attention of Sol LeWitt, who befriended Darboven and became an early champion of her work, which had certain affinities with his conceptual art.

Over time, Darboven came to use numbers in a new way. The realization that the numbers designating dates on the Gregorian calendar could serve as a neutral, "graphic equivalent for the basically nonvisual phenomenon of time" allowed her to engage in the satisfying act of writing without describing.[4] Thus by the late 1960s, the chronicle of time, manifest in Darboven's daily commitment to writing the date in various forms (numerals, words) and based on an ever-evolving system of her own making, became the defining aspect of her art praxis. She also incorporated into many of her works the German word "heute," meaning "today," which she crossed out to depict the transformation of the present into the past.

In 1973, Darboven started including texts by various authors, among them Heinrich Heine and Jean-Paul Sartre, in her work. By 1978, she was also incorporating visual documents such as photographic images and assorted objects that she found, purchased, or received as gifts. These additional elements allowed her to explore specific and varied aspects of time and history—including an abstract version of biography—even as she remained faithful to her personal formal and conceptual approach. In the late 1970s, Darboven, who had studied to be a pianist earlier in life, began to devise a system of musical notation based on the

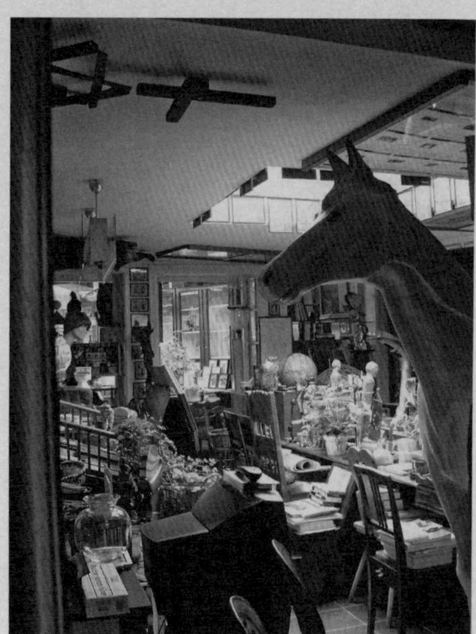

HANNE DARBOVEN'S HOME, 2004

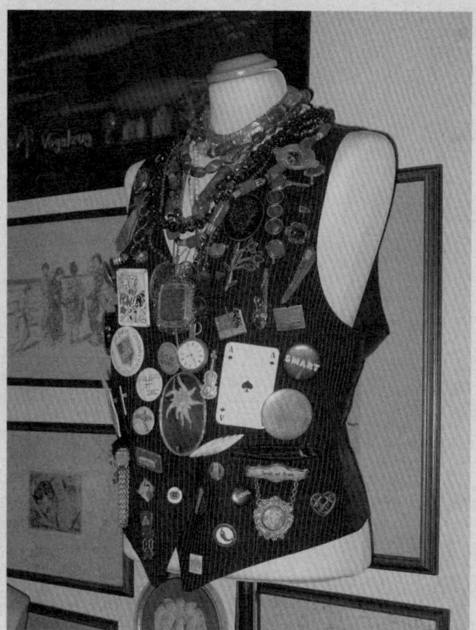

HANNE DARBOVEN'S VEST, 2005

calendar and her personal number systems, and, with the aid of a collaborator, adapted her autographs into performable compositions. Music, an inherently temporal medium, provided Darboven with a new means of enhancing the visual artwork that is the core of her oeuvre. Thus, by the end of this decade, she had begun to develop all of the elements that came to characterize the "Hanne Darboven" style.

MASTERING THE MASTER

In the 1990s, Darboven found herself over half a century into her life and more than thirty years into her career. During this final decade before the turn of the millennium, end-of-the-century rhetoric was prevalent in the cultural conversation. As an artist totally focused on time and deeply committed to the theme of the century, Darboven naturally turned her attention to what that moment meant for her personally, and on a more universal level what one could say about art in the twentieth century. She decided to produce a fin de siècle installation that engaged both her signature mode of marking time through the systematic writing of numbers and an investigation of a common theme of the 1990s, the recognition of archetypal individuals seen to represent the last one hundred years. She knew that only one person could be thought to embody twentieth-century art: Pablo Picasso.

In 1995, Darboven began work on *Hommage à Picasso*, which followed in the vein of an earlier work that combined the theme of the century with a secondary focus on a prominent historical figure. In 1971, she produced *Ein Jahrhundert* (*A Century*), which visualized the hundred-year span through numbers representing each day and year, starting with the 00 and ending in 99. Omitting the first two

digits of the year, themselves the marker of the century, she made the work less about the specific period than the passage of time in general. But she did link the piece to a historical figure, and hence a specific time period, through the work's subtitle, "Dedicated to Johann Wolfgang von Goethe." In placing the memorialized figure at the center of her homage to the century, Darboven raised the issue of how an artist's work is read and interpreted across time.

Moreover, the work itself evolved over time. In 1982, on the occasion of the 150th anniversary of Goethe's death, Darboven added various new elements to the original piece, among them a fifty-one-page text section that included an encyclopedia entry on the writer, as well as Darboven's numeric documentation of all 150 anniversaries of his death date.[5] In 1999, Darboven added a plaster cast of the famous *Bust of Goethe* (1820) by Christian Daniel Rauch.

Hommage à Picasso, the first version of which was completed around the same time as the third iteration of the Goethe piece, also features a bust of its subject. When Darboven conceived of the project, she decided to show a sculpted image of Picasso in a later stage of his life, when his fame had reached its zenith but the originality of his art was greatly diminished. She enlisted the help of Hamburg-based conservator Thomas Fey in locating a suitable work. When he was unable to find one, Fey asked his sister Inge Polynice, a sculptor, to make a maquette of such a representation. Darboven loved Polynice's bust (see page 49), whose distinguished face recalls the sculpted portraits of Roman emperors, writers, philosophers, and the like, and she elected to incorporate a bronze version of it into the installation.

Just as the bust indicated an emphasis on Picasso's later years, so, too, did another object in the installation, which served as a major point of departure for Darboven's overall concept: a lithograph of Picasso's 1955 painting *Seated Figure in Turkish Costume* (see page 15). When Darboven acquired this lithograph, it came in a hand-painted, wooden frame with abstract black, blue, and yellow shapes on a white ground that mimicked the palette of the painting and was reminiscent of Picasso's Cubism. This Picasso-esque frame demonstrates how the most distinctive elements of an artist's work can be extracted, deconstructed, and reused in ways that have little relation to the original source. Darboven's fascination with this pastiche, which in many senses trivialized Picasso's formal innovations, led her to research the frame's origins. She discovered that it had been hand painted in Poland and subsequently commissioned 270 similar, though slightly larger, replicas for the date panels she was producing for the installation. In this way, she combined her own handwritten, "original" work with hand-painted frames that were simultaneously the "unique" products of individual, albeit anonymous, artisans and an invocation of the revered, mystified hand of Picasso.

Darboven's date panels for *Hommage à Picasso* contain an incredible 9,720 sheets of paper. In total, they constitute a tangible account of the daily effort she expended during 1995–96 to complete this component of the installation. The pages document the 1990s, the last decade of the twentieth century and the demarcation of the fin de siècle, a subject she has frequently explored over the years. As always, she represented the year only via the last two digits (thus the precise century that this final decade belongs to is unspecified). Each frame holds thirty-six A4-sized (the standard letter size outside the U.S. and Canada) parchment sheets with numbers handwritten in felt-tip pen according to one of four distinct systems for representing time. In the first grouping, which consists of 120 panels, each sheet presents a single day with the date handwritten four times vertically, and each panel is comprised of all the sheets for a single month. The second group, which contains 60 panels, follows a similar format; however, the numbers are laid out horizontally and each panel represents two months. The third set, also containing 60 panels—each of which represents two months—uses words instead of numerals to document the dates vertically. And each of the final 30 panels documents four months, with the date written in words horizontally. The numeric writing on every sheet follows a 4 x 4 square format that recalls the influence of artists such as Piet Mondrian, Kazimir Malevich, and Josef Albers on Darboven's early work and her *Konstruktionen* of the mid-1960s.

While the artist chose to invoke the genesis of her distinctive style with this formal choice, her decision to include a portrait of an elder Picasso and her selection of a work from the 1950s, *Seated Figure in Turkish Costume*, stressed Picasso's later, less groundbreaking work in order to interrogate the role of repetition and citation in his art. During this decade, Picasso began a series of paraphrased pictures that responded to work by other artists, for example, Eugene Delacroix and Edouard Manet. *Seated Figure* depicts Picasso's lover Jacqueline Roque in the exuberant palette and exotic costume of Henri Matisse's odalisques, which themselves owe a debt to Ingres's paintings of Turkish baths. Picasso painted a number of similar works shortly after Matisse's

death, and in certain respects they function as an elegy or homage to his late friend.

Picasso nonetheless put his personal stamp on the subject through the use of his own signature style. By the 1950s, the Picasso style had come to signify modern art in the popular imagination. The accessibility and widespread usage of his semi-abstract Cubism robbed it of its originality and avant-garde status, as did the artist's practice of continuously recycling and repeating old motifs and formal approaches. Moreover, the sources of Picasso's innovation had themselves been lost in translation. His appropriation of the formal language of other cultures' anonymous, indigenous artwork—principally, African masks and sculpture—had largely been overshadowed by the myth of his genius and his central role in the radical transformation of the Western art-historical tradition.

Indeed, the Picasso-esque, Polish-made frames in Darboven's piece involve a reversal of Picasso's method. The unknown artisans deconstructed his

visual codes and transformed them back into something anonymous. Contrary to Picasso's use of abstract form to produce figurative works, they produced non-objective, nonrepresentational compositions. In this sense, the artisans provide the perfect frame for Darboven's conceptual art, which runs counter to the tradition of representational painting that Picasso continued to operate within despite his use of an abstract visual vocabulary. In separating the frames from the Picasso lithograph, Darboven obscures their "homage" almost beyond recognition.

In the installation, Darboven also included a more concrete motif that raises issues about the interpretation of an artist's oeuvre over time: the goat. Like the lithograph of *Seated Figure*, the inclusion of a bronze sculpture of a goat (see page 51) by Wolfgang Binding invokes a later-career Picasso piece, his sculpted *She-Goat* of 1950. During the 1950s, Picasso produced a number of works that included representations of a goat—many of them in materials not

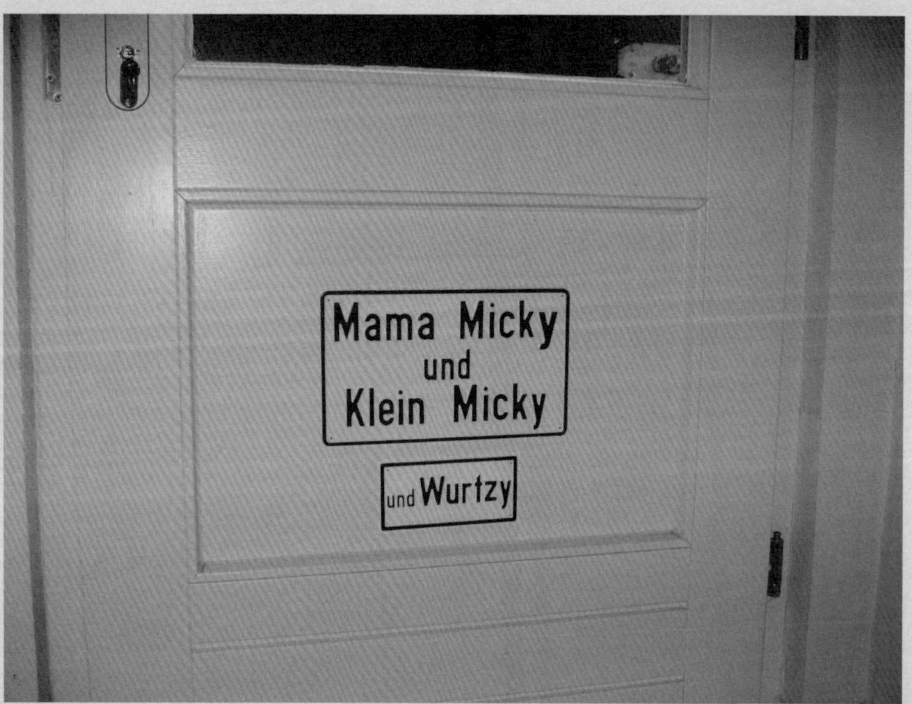

DOOR IN HANNE DARBOVEN'S HOME, 2004

usually associated with high art such as ceramics and mixed media—including the original version of *She-Goat*, a playful sculptural assemblage composed of such nonart materials as a palm leaf, flowerpots, a wicker basket, strips of metal, and fragments of plaster. Picasso also made two bronze casts of this latter work, which are now in the collections of the Musée Picasso, Paris, and the Museum of Modern Art, New York.

In the early twentieth century, Picasso played a pioneering role in the use of found, everyday materials in fine artworks. By incorporating such nontraditional mediums as newsprint and oilcloth into his Cubist collages, he blurred the border between high and low in art and significantly expanded the formal options for artists. While the prototype for *She-Goat* straddled this boundary line, it is the bronze version that attained an iconic status, codified in the art-historical canon in large part due to its prominent display in the sculpture garden of the Museum of Modern Art. Darboven alludes to the aura of the bronze "original" through the inclusion of Binding's expressionist bronze goat, which has evident affinities with Picasso's work. However, Binding's method has much more in common with traditional academic models of high art than with the innovative collage technique that imbues Picasso's *She-Goat* with its humorous, distinctive, visual character.

Darboven contrasts the goat with three birch-twig donkeys (see page 55) made by Polish folk artists. The donkeys represent a subject often associated with Spain, Picasso's country of origin, yet they, like the painted frames, come from Poland and have no identifiable author. Similar to Picasso's goat assemblage, they employ materials not usually associated with fine art to create an abstract representation of an animal. However, the donkeys are not accorded the special value and recognition that Picasso's goat has received precisely because of their association with the anonymous, folk-art tradition. Through the donkeys, Darboven underscores the point that the identity of the maker plays a major role in imbuing a work with significance; without this marker of meaning, works of art are not included in history books.

A large part of history's obsession with the individuals who shape it is the fascination with the role of biography in their lifework. Ironically, Darboven's inclusion of the goat motif links her to Picasso, as both artists had pet goats who served as muses and subjects for their art. Picasso made many works depicting goats in the early 1950s, when he kept a pet goat named Esmeralda in his house in the south of France. Darboven also has a pet goat, Micky, who is both companion and artistic collaborator. There have been a number of Mickys through the years, as well as one goat, the baby of one of the Mickys, named Wurtzy. The fact that Darboven has used the same name for most of her goats seems consistent with her work's emphasis on repetition, slight variation, universal archetypes, and the passage of time. The importance of time is underscored by the presence in her backyard of a plaque commemorating the deceased Mickys, as well as by the taxidermied Mickys displayed in her home-cum-museum. Darboven repeatedly signs her works "H.D. and Micky," thereby crediting the pet's inspiration and collaboration.

Micky has also literally been part of her work, as in the case of *Existenz 66-88*, (1989, *Existence 66-88*). Considered by many to be a self-portrait, the installation consists of photos of the pages of Darboven's personal date book, which chronicle her daily activities and interactions from 1966 to 1988. She also included one of the stuffed Mickys, thereby emphasizing the importance of her beloved goat in both her daily life and her art. More recently, she produced the installation *Hanneles Tierleben* (1988–90, *Little Hanne's Animal Life*) based on a

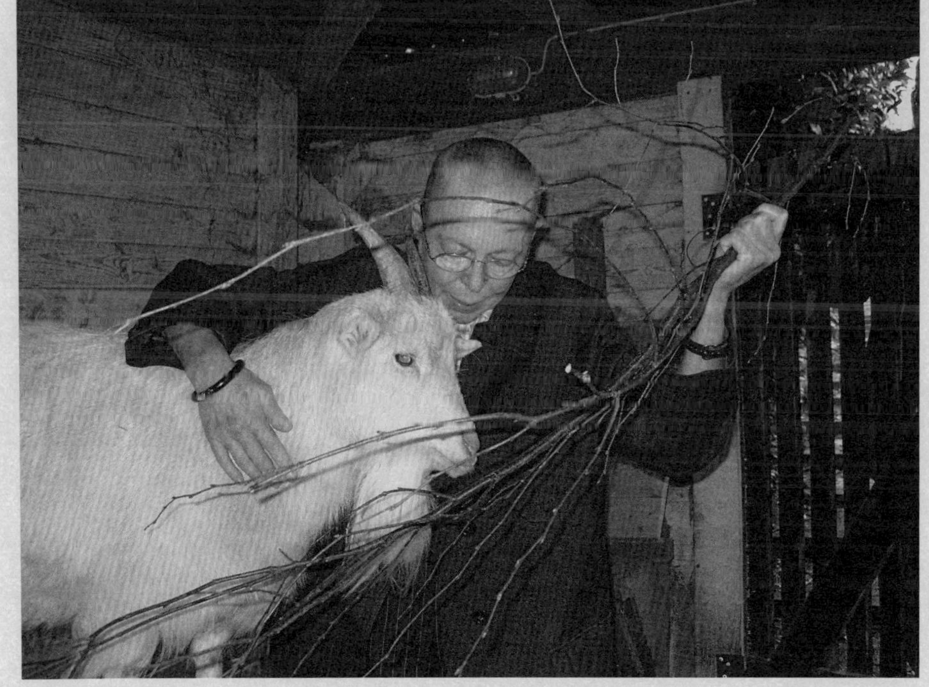

HANNE DARBOVEN AND MICKY, 2005

book about goat breeding, in which she framed each double-sided page from the book.[6] Through such works, Darboven, like Picasso and other artists, repeats and reinvents her signature style and common themes time and again.

But the notion of recycling and reinterpretation is not just thematized by *Hommage à Picasso*; Darboven has in fact literalized this concept by producing two iterations of the work. When first exhibited at the Deichtorhallen in Hamburg from November 1999 to February 2000—a span of time that coincided with the turn of the twentieth century[7]—*Hommage à Picasso* contained several items in addition to the panels and the three-dimensional objects in the present installation: several other reproductions of late Picassos; a porcelain parrot whose colors match those of *Seated Figure*; a life-sized human model; and a candle from 1873 depicting fictional historical figures.[8]

These items placed a strong emphasis on the mimetic art tradition out of which Picasso developed and which continued to exert an influence on his work throughout his lengthy career. Darboven contrasts this approach with her conceptual art, manifest in her numeric text panels, which does not attempt to represent the natural world. In drawing this comparison between her work and that of the old masters, Picasso included, she calls attention to fundamental changes that art has undergone since the middle of the twentieth century. By emphasizing Picasso's work in the 1950s, she shows that the artist regarded as the greatest genius of the twentieth century ultimately could not move beyond either his own signature style and usual subjects, or the art of the past, as exemplified by his exhaustive series of the late 1950s

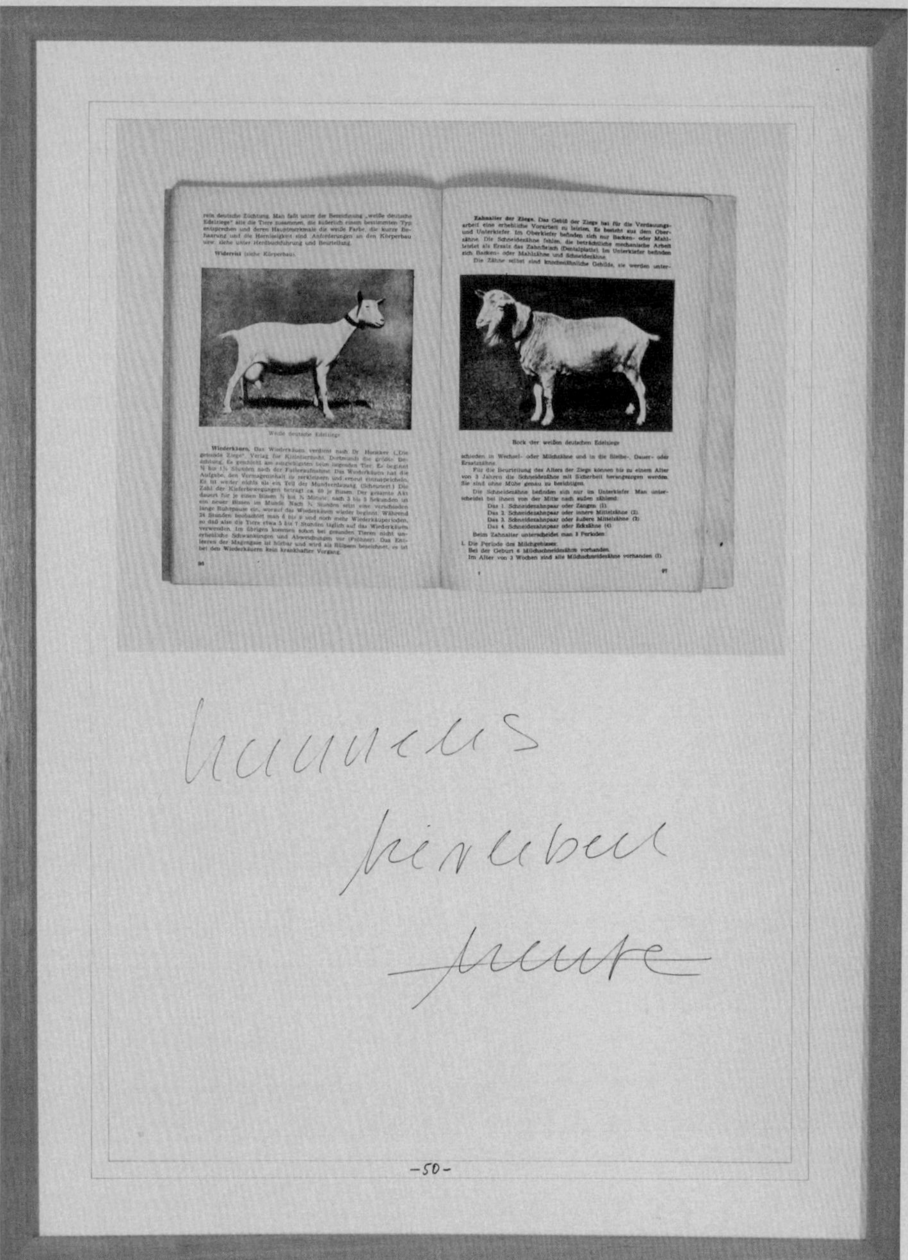

FRAMED DOUBLE-SIDED PAGE FROM HANNE DARBOVEN, *HANNELES TIERLEBEN*, 1988–90

based on Diego Velázquez's masterpiece *Las Meninas*.

One final element in Darboven's installation further drives home this point: a set of two vitrines, each containing six sculptures of the signs of the zodiac (see page 53). These works are sold by the Hannover-based commercial company ars mundi (Die Welt der Kunst), which specializes in museum reproductions and works inspired by famous paintings and sculptures. In its promotional materials for these sculptures, ars mundi describes the artist, Meta Morfosi, as following in the tradition of Picasso's assemblages— and indeed the sculptures are visually reminiscent of his work. Like the Picasso lithograph in *Hommage à Picasso*, which was sold with a written guarantee of quality, Morfosi's zodiac sculptures are editioned, signed, and promised to be authentic. While one could certainly argue that Morfosi's works are "original" on the grounds they are not copies of specific Picasso works, the end result is fundamentally rooted in a commercialized, kitschy interpretation of the Picasso style, which in no way constitutes a radical formal transformation—or meta-morphosis—as the artist's somewhat humorous moniker implies.[9] In the context of Darboven's installation, the zodiac signs testify to the fact that at the end of the twentieth century, Picasso's art had been stripped of its radicalism and largely reduced to sterile, clichéd reproductions and pop culture adaptations.

PLAY IT AGAIN AND AGAIN

With *Hommage à Picasso*, Darboven confronts the meaning and significance of the use of repetition and citation. Her homage to Picasso certainly comments upon the Spaniard's work, but even more so, it paints a picture of her own art and praxis. Through the lens of Picasso's life and work, Darboven considers how her later-career work will stand the test of time and judgment of history. Like Picasso, she has a readily identifiable signature style; when one sees a work on paper with numbers arranged in a seemingly systematic way, the name Hanne Darboven immediately comes to mind. Also like Picasso, each of her works exhibits slight variations in theme and composition: she combines the numbers in different ways, for instance, or employs various formal means of arranging and displaying them.

But as the last major aspect of this installation—produced especially for this commission—attests, Darboven has found a way to transform, or metamorphose, her work through the fundamentally temporal medium of music. She composed Opus 60, a piece for 120 instruments, and the musicologist Wolfgang Marx then transposed her autograph into a musical score, a recording of which constitutes an integral part of *Hommage à Picasso*.[10] As with Darboven's previous musical works, Opus 60 chronicles a set period of time, but in contrast to the numeric text panels of *Hommage à Picasso*, which document only the last ten years of the twentieth century, Opus 60 incorporates every day of the hundred-year span. The piece takes time (to perform and listen to) and also represents it. Moreover, it transforms Darboven's concept of repetition from a formal, mostly visual articulation into a sensuous musical experience. With her music, Darboven has managed to produce a wholly abstract art, devoid of references to the material world and independent of physical forms.

Hommage à Picasso simultaneously acknowledges that Picasso was the last great painter of the twentieth century and argues that the repetitiveness of his late work—and its legacy in the decades following his death—revealed the limitations of the medium and the traditional approach to visual art as expression that he still utilized. Darboven cleverly contrasts this analytical portrait of Picasso with a conceptual picture of her own approach. Like the Spanish master, she continuously repeats and reinterprets the defining elements of her personal style. But she has transcended the constraints of monotonous visual citations by developing her music, which is at once clearly identifiable as Hanne Darboven's work and indicative of the limitless possibilities of her oeuvre as a whole to reinvent itself time and again.

Notes

1   For more on Darboven's daily numeric writing, which constitutes the foundation of her artistic praxis, see Anne Rorimer, "Numbering the Days: Hanne Darboven's Calendar Work," on pages 13—14 of this catalogue.

2   The original painting is in the collection of the Hamburger Kunsthalle, Darboven's local museum.

3   For an excellent account of Darboven's early work, I would refer the reader to *Hanne Darboven: Das Frühwerk* (Hamburg: Hamburger Kunsthalle, 1999).

4   Klaus Honnef, "Art Encyclopedias of Culture: Klaus Honnef on Hanne Darboven," in *Hanne Darboven: Primitive Zeit/Uhrzeit, Primitive Time/Clock Time*, exh. brochure (Philadelphia: Goldie Paley Gallery, Moore College of Art and Design, 1990), p. 7.

5   For a more detailed account of this work, I would refer the reader to Mario Kramer, *Hanne Darboven: Ein Jahrhundert—Johann Wolfgang von Goethe, 1971–82*, exh. pamphlet (Frankfurt am Main: Museum für Moderne Kunst Frankfurt am Main, n.d.).

6   This show was held at the Galerie Elisabeth Kaufmann, Zurich, from January 10 to February 28, 2003.

7   The exhibition ran from November 19, 1999 to February 27, 2000.

8   For more on this work, I would refer the reader to the Deichtorhallen's press release for the exhibition.

9   I am grateful to my colleague David Grosz for calling my attention to this point.

10 For more on the Darboven/Marx collaboration and the genesis of Opus 60, see Wolfgang Marx, "'A Section of Something That Has Eternally Begun and Will Continue to Sound Forever': Hanne Darboven's Time Music," on pages 69—73 of this catalogue.

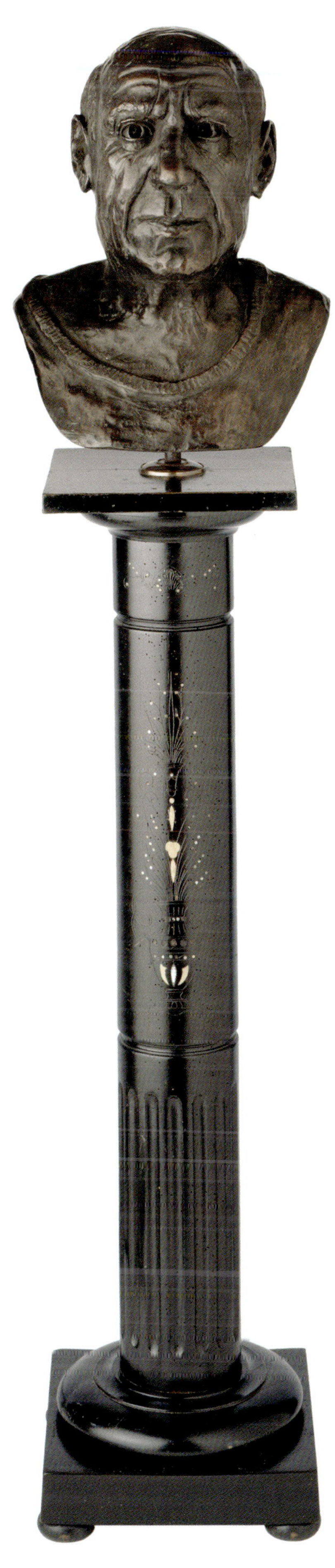

Bust of Picasso, by Inge Polynice,
from Hanne Darboven, *Hommage
à Picasso*, 1995–2006. Bronze,
edition 2/8, 151 × 33.5 × 29 cm overall.

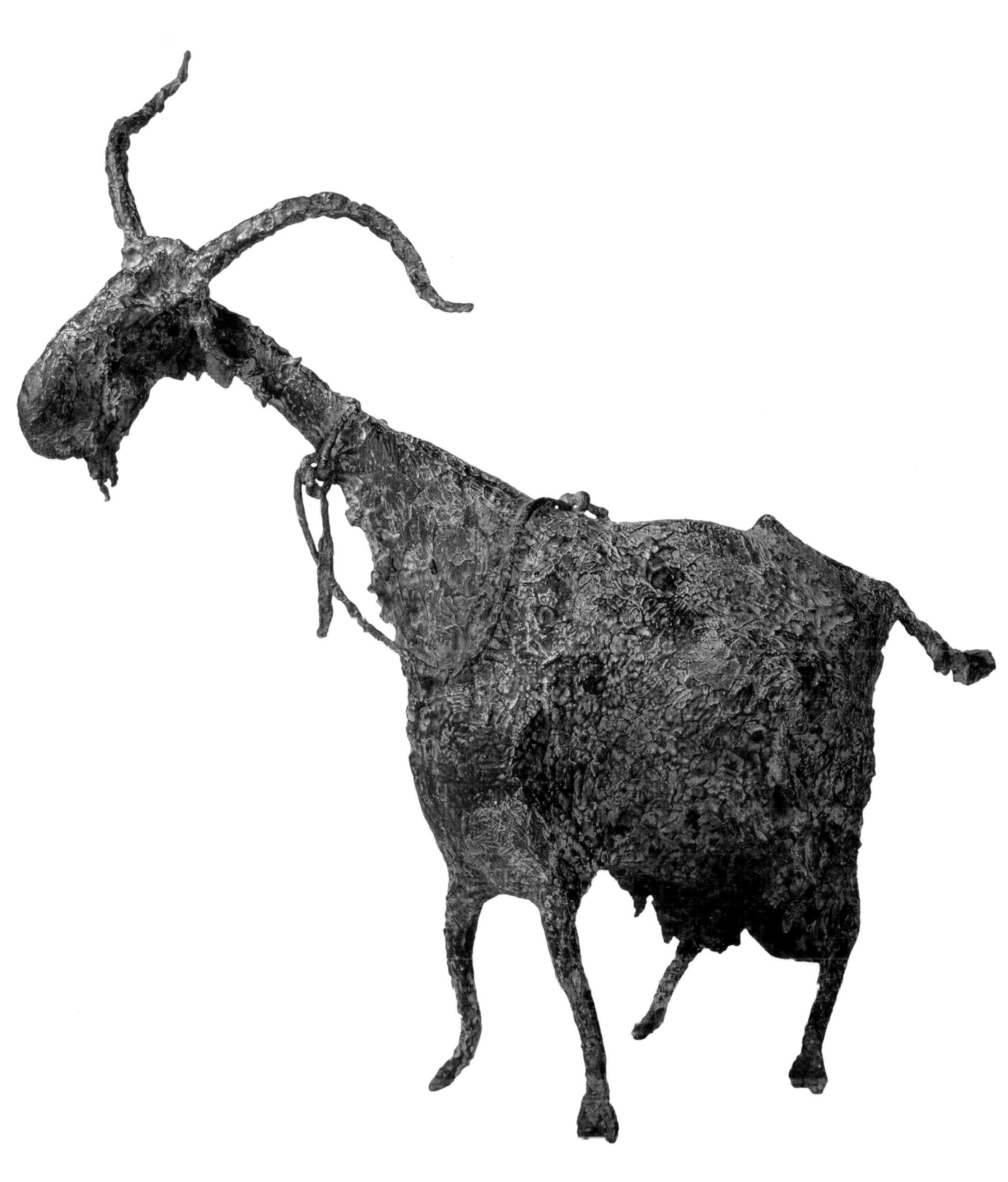

Goat, by Wolfgang Binding, from
Hanne Darboven, *Hommage à Picasso*,
1995–2006. Bronze, 120 × 124 × 42 cm.

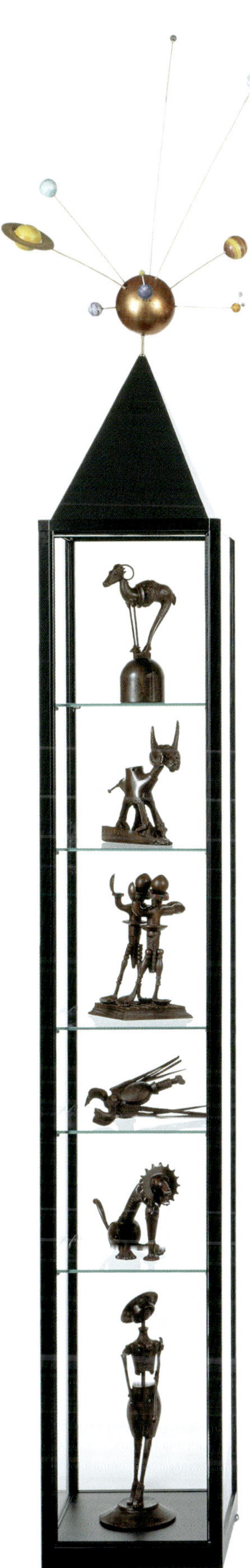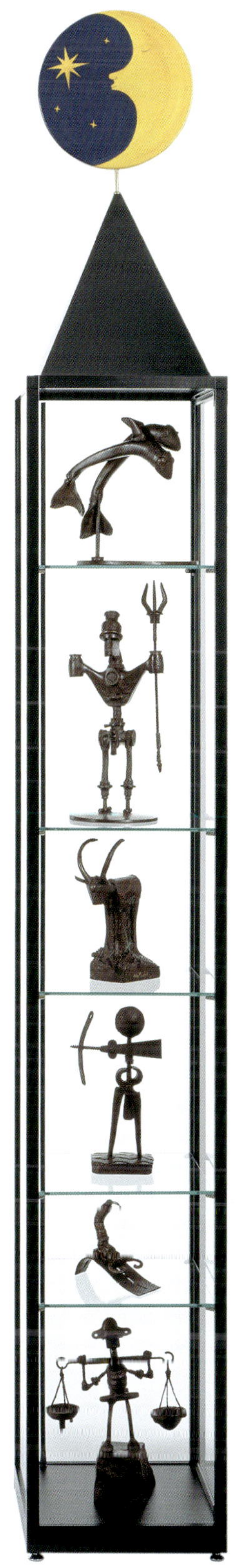

Twelve signs of the zodiac, by
Meta Morfosi, from Hanne Darboven,
Hommage à Picasso, 1995–2006.
Polished and patinated cast metal,
with two vitrines, 201.5 × 35 × 35 cm
each vitrine.

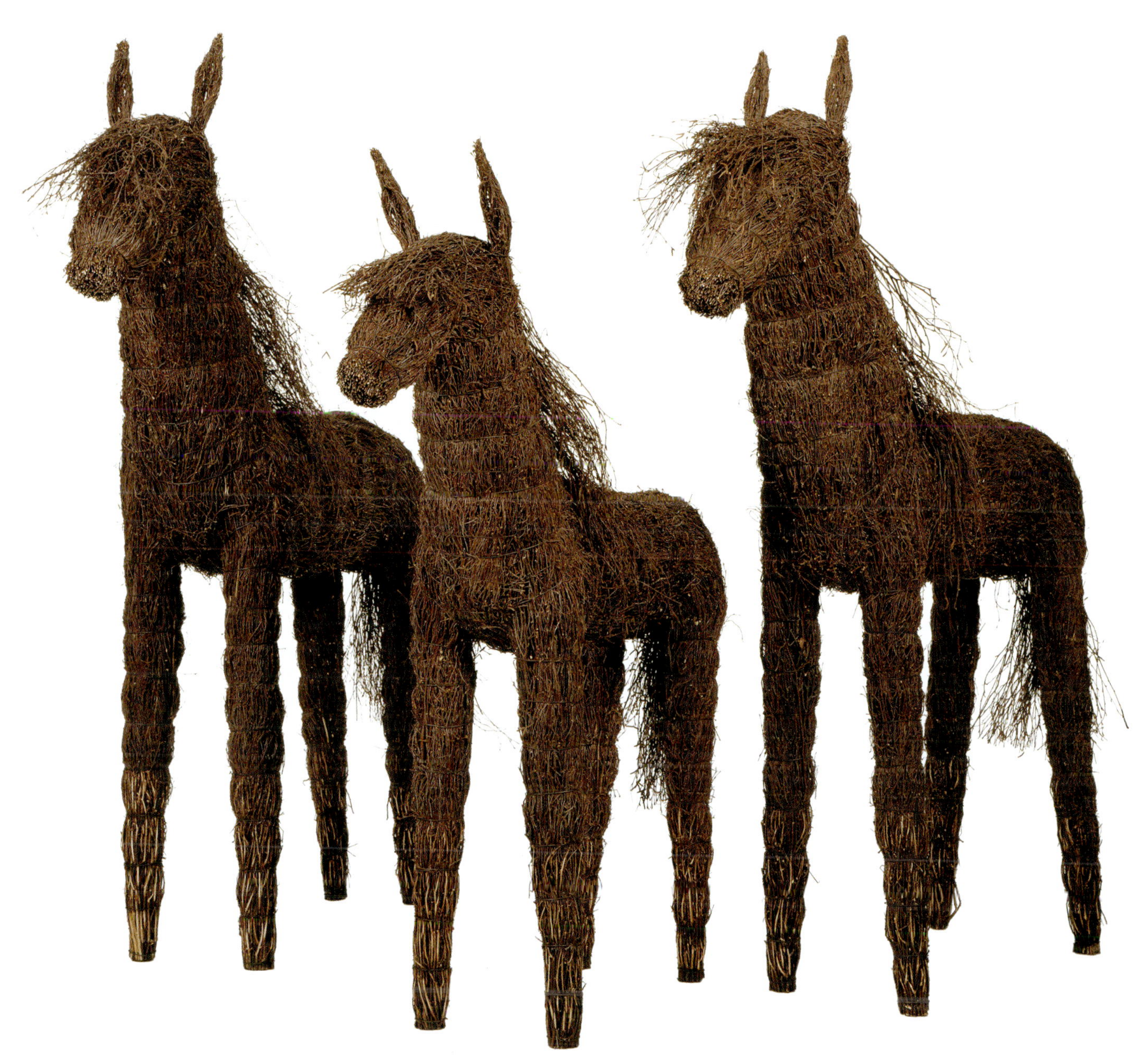

Three donkeys, craftwork from Poland,
from Hanne Darboven, *Hommage à
Picasso*, 1995–2006. Birch twigs,
169 × 143 × 43 cm; 196 × 173 × 45 cm; and
200 × 173 × 44 cm.

Hanne Darboven: My Work Ends in Music
Gerd de Vries with Sibylle Omlin

ON OCTOBER 3 AND 4, 2003, THE HAUS KONSTRUKTIV, ZURICH, HOSTED THE DEBUT PERFORMANCE OF HANNE DARBOVEN'S WIND QUINTET, OP. 42. ON THE OCCASION OF THE EVENT, INDEPENDENT ART CRITIC AND CURATOR SIBYLLE OMLIN TALKED WITH MUSICOLOGIST GERD DE VRIES, THE CODIRECTOR OF THE FORMER GALERIE PAUL MAENZ, COLOGNE. THE EDITED TRANSCRIPT OF THE INTERVIEW IS PRINTED HERE FOR THE FIRST TIME.

SIBYLLE OMLIN: It is obvious that Hanne Darboven's artistic work, which begins with writing and calculating, is trying to extend more and more into space. On the one hand, space in her work tends to be abstract (she records history and time-space with numerical data), but on the other hand it takes on more and more of a physical component, by extending into the exhibition space and also, nowadays, through the acoustic means of music. What does music mean to her work and the development of her artistic language?

GERD DE VRIES: First, perhaps, a few basic remarks about Hanne Darboven's musical system. The first reference to it is found in her work *Aufzeichnung: Kosmos >85<* (1985–86, *Record: Cosmos*).[1] Essentially, it goes like this: in the classic notation system, the staff, there are five lines and four spaces, a total of nine specified areas. A tenth area can stand either above or below the staff. The result: I can express all the single-digit numbers (0 through 9) in musical notes. Several different possibilities are available, for example, placing the 1 at the bottom and numbering upward (in Darboven's system that is the A form; in it, 1 = E, 2 = F, 3 = G, etc.) or placing the 1 at the top and numbering downward (the B form; in traditional parlance this would be the "inversion" of the

A form, where 1 = F, 2 = E, 3 = D, etc.). Moreover, I can play the sequences of notes either as a melody or a chord. So I have four different possibilities for organizing the same numbers. Essentially a very simple, but at the same time quite ingenious invention for translating numbers into music. (The system is then further expanded in detail: for two-digit numbers like 10, 20, 30, etc., the first number is expressed by a triad, the zero by a 6/4 chord.)

All of Darboven's musical works are based on number constructions (what she calls "number scores"), that is, calculations of the sums of the digits in calendar dates. (Interestingly enough, the large work in the Museum für Moderne Kunst in Frankfurt is called *Ein Jahrhundert— Johann Wolfgang von Goethe gewidmet* (1971–82, *A Century—Dedicated to Johann Wolfgang von Goethe*), but when it was transformed into a musical score, op. 25, it was given the title *Ludwig van Beethoven.*

Even in the numerical work there are various parallel ways of presenting her dates, her "constructions"—they usually involve calculating the time-space of a century.[2] In addition, there are various ways to represent a number graphically. A digit, say 5, can be expressed by five boxes or five U-shapes or—reflecting its numerical value—written out five times: as digits "5 5 5 5 5," as the number name "five five five five five," or as a rising sequence "one two three four five." That is: I can "paraphrase" time, "describe" it visually, in different ways.

Which part of such calculations, such constructions, is to be used for a musical work is then determined based on compositional considerations. Depending on the original number, the composition will be shorter or longer (the twelve sections of her Chamber Symphony, op. 27, total roughly fifteen minutes of playing time;

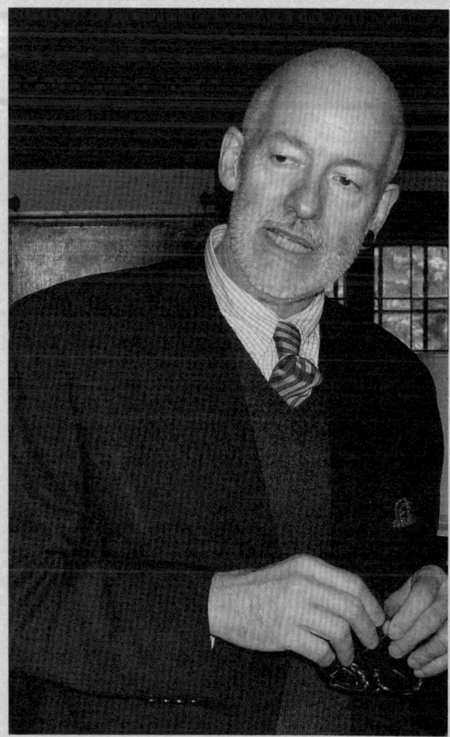

GERD DE VRIES, 2004

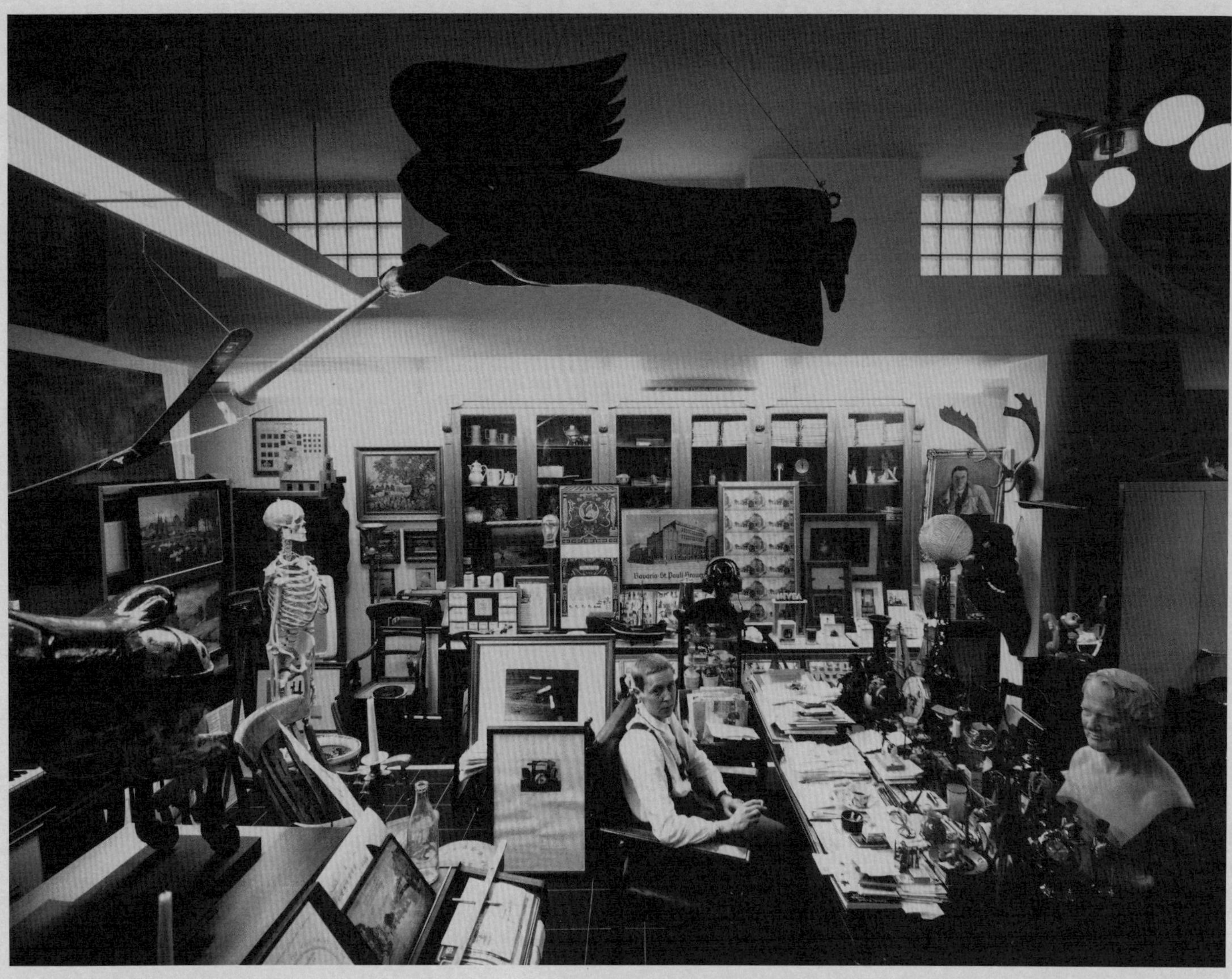

HANNE DARBOVEN IN HER STUDIO, 1987

the forty-two sections of her Harp Solo, op. 45, last six or seven hours).

Darboven writes the numbers she has decided on—corresponding to their position in the system—as notes on her special music paper (with the above-mentioned numbered lines and spaces) in a very simple notation, without bar lines, without anything other than the notes. When the church musician Friedrich Stoppa began working for her around 1979–80, converting her originals into a score that musicians might play—it was very precise, as if printed, worked out on a computer—he would faithfully transpose what she had written out for him, each mark into a note. This is the case in Opera 1–18.

He then wondered whether one could not create a kind of "melodic voice" to go with the uniform structure of the music— and that would develop out of it. He did so for the first time in Requiem for Organ, op. 19, where a flute can be added to the organ as a solo instrument if desired. You could compare this to the Bach/Gounod "Ave Maria" (the first prelude of the first book of Bach's *Well-Tempered Clavier*, to which Gounod added a singable melody— again above the uniform structure of the music). With Darboven's permission, Stoppa's "free" voices became in time freer and freer, until we reach the String Sextet, op. 44, in which in my opinion Darboven's original structure is scarcely recognizable.

In early music the fundamental structure was the so-called *cantus firmus*, a Gregorian melody, above which a musical structure was erected. Something similar happened later in Renaissance music, where entire masses were based on specific chansons, other masses, or sections or movements from them. An external pattern then determined the whole structure, and it was usually heard as well. But the other, overlying texture was much more dominant, of course, and more clearly occupied the foreground (this was the true creation of the given composer). It seems to me that in Stoppa's last scores for Darboven, his texture dominates Darboven's ground structure. Whereas for me, in the genuine "Hanne

Darboven," a perfectly dry, pure, simple progression is what is most exciting, because there her principle is most effective. It is this naked, direct form of rising and falling number sequences that is represented in equally naked music (for example, rising D-E, D-F, D-G, D-A, etc.).

SO: But Darboven is no longer working with Stoppa, who has meanwhile died. Now her collaborator is Wolfgang Marx. Surely you have heard more recent compositions of her work. How are they going?

GDV: It seems to me that now there is more genuine "Hanne Darboven" again, as in the Harp Solo, op. 45, for example. On the other hand, some of the new compositions have taken on very large forms. Marx is currently working on the transcription of a symphony for 120 voices (Opus 60, which accompanies this exhibition)—that is an extremely large orchestra. Darboven chooses the instruments, in close consultation with Marx, of course. He is a young and very exciting musical scholar, a professor at University College Dublin.[3]

SO: So this means that the musical works have returned to the genuine "Hanne Darboven" and we can once again hear the original?

GDV: That is a very broad question. At first, Darboven wrote only number constructions, the simple sums of digits in calendar dates or their graphic translation in the form of U-shapes/wavy lines, little boxes, etc. At that time—we are talking about 1968 or so—some people accused her of "abstract art," *l'art pour l'art*. She protested vehemently: "That is utter nonsense. All these dates that I work with, every date, for that matter, is naturally filled with history." (Darboven is one of the most politically aware people I know, by the way.)

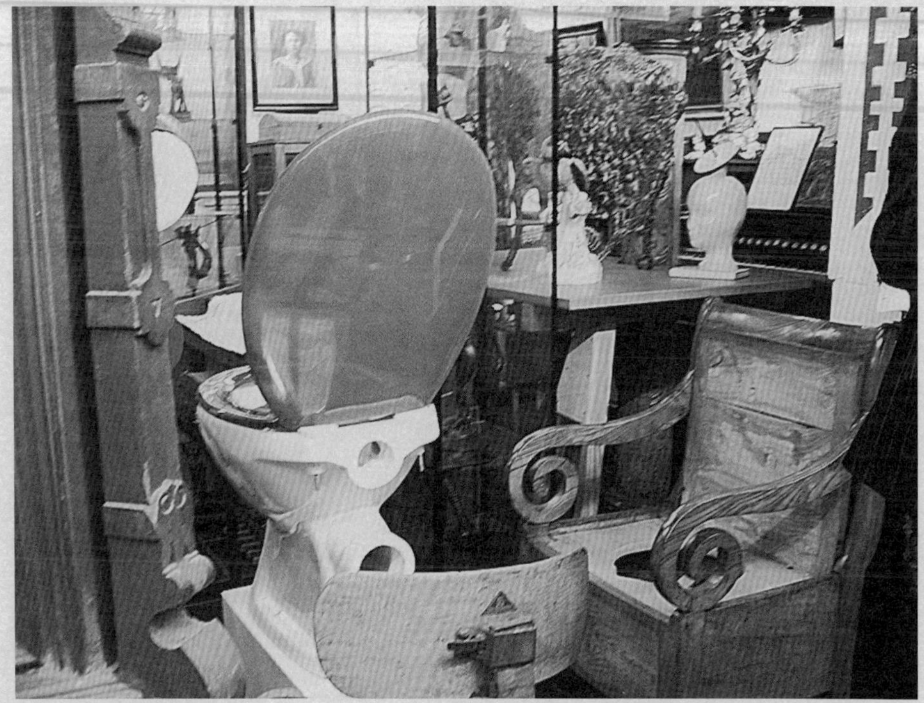

HANNE DARBOVEN'S HOME, 2004

To explain how this relates to the real world, in the 1970s she began to include photographs, postcards, and other visual elements in her works (in exhibitions she arranged actual objects from the vast collection she had meanwhile assembled). These could be—as in *Cultural History*—covers from *Der Spiegel* for an entire year or pages from Werner Stein's *Kulturfahrplan* (*Timetables of History*), basically anything that you could imagine. In *Ost-West-Demokratie* (1983, *East-West Democracy*), flags of the East and West German Republics; in *Bismarckzeit* (1978, *Age of Bismarck*), a statue of Bismarck with his dog, but also porcelain plates with corny sayings like "One crazy person is normal, when two people are crazy watch out," or "Work ennobles—I'd rather stay bourgeois." It got as low as that; her horizon is truly very broad. But in *Age of Bismarck* there were also long excerpts she had copied out of the *Brockhaus Encyclopedia*, entries about Bismarck's "social legislation," biographical details, and more.

Which means: her art is highly aware, very intense, and extremely artistic in its subject. But some of the examples she includes in *Cultural History* are objects of the utmost banality: amusement-park swans, prostheses from World War I, Art Nouveau chamber pots, ceramic Elvis Presley figures, the Brandenburg Gate made out of chocolate . . . the selection is truly broad. And it is the viewer's job to make sense out of it. Not as in Bertolt Brecht, who always tells you what you are supposed to think. Instead Darboven spreads out her panorama and says: "There's this and this and that—now it's up to you. I'm not going to dictate how you're supposed to think. But if you have any sense at all, you'll have to draw the same conclusions I do. But that's your business." Her system is very open. Everything, truly everything, the most exalted and the most mundane, can find a place in and serve as an example for her *Kulturgeschichte, Weltansichten, Welttheater, Evolution, Existenz. . . .*[4]

SO: And this openness also plays a role in her music, in her collaboration with the person who reformulates her notations musically?

GDV: I think so. Even a piece like the String Sextet, op. 44, which in my opinion strays far from the genuine "Hanne Darboven," can in this respect be annexed without difficulties, precisely like any other object. As caesuras between individual sections in the early compositions, there are various "intermezzi": "Silent Night, Holy Night" or John Lennon and Yoko Ono's "Give Peace a Chance" in Opera 1–6; Edith Piaf singing "Non, je ne regrette rien" in Opus 14; or Bach's Toccata in D-Minor (BWV 565, which according to the most recent scholarship is not actually his) in Opera 19–22.

SO: You are a music historian, and you have said that Darboven's system is an ingenious invention. Can you classify it and evaluate it in terms of music history?

GDV: Not exactly classify it. It is so unusual, so unique . . . there hasn't been anything like it before, that's why I find it so exciting. I have always been interested in things like this that fall out of the usual framework, what you might call "extramusical methods." In Renaissance music it was quite common to adopt extramusical motifs. There's the famous mass by Josquin, for example, *Hercules Dux Ferrariae*. From this dedication, "Hercules, Duke of Ferrara," the composer derived the corresponding musical tones—following the names for the notes of the scale then in use, that is to say, Ut, Re, Mi, Fa, Sol, La—which then served as the basis for the composition. The first "e" in "Hercules" became a "Re" (corresponding to a D in our system), the "u" became an "Ut" (our C), the second "e" another "Re," and so on.

Composers would extract from words a basic musical foundation—a kind of *cantus firmus*—on which they erected a musical structure. It was a wholly arbitrary, extramusical procedure. The musical form

is not generated through "development," as in Beethoven—i.e., it begins with a theme, which is then manipulated (the famous sequence of "exposition," "development," "reprise")—but out of the wholly arbitrary decision to take something—in this case, a dedication—as the basis for a composition.

Baroque musicians made considerable use of so-called "rhetorical figures" (that is, specific catchwords in the text—"pain," "rage," "love," "sadness"—triggered specific musical phrases) and also number symbolism. Bach has many good examples of both approaches. Schumann scholars have discovered that their composer developed a system whereby he could extend the series of "musical" letters beyond G and assign a note to every other letter of the alphabet. Accordingly, some of his compositions can be read like texts.

The idea of using something extramusical as the basis for a composition is therefore nothing new. In recent decades, John Cage frequently used such methods, for example in his *Music of Changes*, which is based on chance and is related to principles of the *I Ching*; or in compositions in which the notes are derived from flaws, spots, and inadvertent marks on the manuscript paper. This is done most successfully in *Atlas Eclipticalis*, where he inscribed staff lines on transparent paper and then placed it on top of a map of the night sky so that the stars became the notes. The stars themselves are virtually transformed into music (truly a kind of *musica coelestis*, which was part of medieval musical theory).[5] Thus it is altogether possible to create music that is not based on the European tradition of exposition and development.

SO: And Hanne Darboven, an artist who works in an extramusical field—the visual

arts—has definitely made an important contribution to this?

GDV: To me it is a very important contribution, yes. As I said, I have always been greatly interested in whatever lies outside the musical mainstream. György Ligeti, for example, who is fascinated by the polyrhythms in the music of pygmies, and incorporates them in a section of his piano études. Or composers who work with microtones, another technique that has no place in the standard European musical tradition. Or Olivier Messiaen, who works with bird songs and the most complex rhythms based on Indian music or Indian musical philosophy. In Darboven's music, I am reminded above all of something like Indian ragas, or Arab *maqamat*, melodic figures on which one improvises in a virtually endless sequence of variations, "playing around" the theme, over and over, each time in a new and different way.

In Darboven compositions, time is structured—but not as in Beethoven, with a beginning and an end, or—as in Berlioz, and later to an extreme in Bruckner—with the layering of various themes to create a grandiose finale effect. The structure of European music is after all quite architectural. Bach's *Art of the Fugue* is an example, or for that matter the music of Bruckner. Both of them are quintessentially European composers: out of various themes in various combinations they ultimately erect a kind of cathedral of sound, where everything is once again piled on top of everything else.

But time can also be structured in another, Darbovian sense. As in Erik Satie, for example, in his *Vexations*, which are supposed to be repeated 864 times (the two-day "premiere" in the 1980s happens to have been organized by Cage), or in his notion of *musique d'ameublement* (which Brian Eno would later take up in his "ambient music"). There is a progression in Darboven's music, in that it naturally begins at some point and stops at another, but it is not one that strives for climaxes, some final effect, drama, or ecstasy. Darboven always says: "I don't want any expression." It is all about the passage of time; something is taking place in time; *time itself* is taking place. Cage once put this very well: "Music fills time most definitively." But all without any drama, no outcries, no Toscas leaping off the Castel Sant'Angelo.

Darboven's musical scores are wholly determined by and dependent upon her "number scores," of course, and for that reason they all have something in common. At the same time it is astonishing how different they can be: the sparse, arid structures of the early opera compared to the seeming sensual riot of the String Sextet, op. 44 (I have already expressed my reservations about this piece); the relentless march of time in her symphony (I can't help but think of "Mars, the Bringer of War" from Gustav Holst's *The Planets*) compared to the relaxed, zenlike calm, the heavenly dripping "on cloud seven" in the Harp Solo, op. 45 (virtually "postcards from heaven," as Cage called one of his compositions); or the *divine longeurs* (Schumann's remark about Schubert's last symphonies) of Requiem for Organ, op. 19, which derive from the fact that specific intervals, corresponding to their numerical value, are frequently repeated, for example A–F (4 and 2 in Darboven's notation) forty-two times. No other composition strikes me as so completely "Hanne Darboven," nor moves me as much, as Opus 19. A remarkable phenomenon, a kind of reversal: the time that was captured, recorded, "concentrated" in her calculations is here spread out again: it disperses, becomes almost "timeless." . . .

Time is unquestionably the real subject in Darboven. In this aspect, she is related to someone like On Kawara. In conjunction with his *Date Paintings*, On Kawara often collects the newspaper of the date in question. He, therefore, does not make "abstract" art; rather a specific date is filled to the brim with "life," just as in Darboven. But she has larger structures of time in mind. On Kawara is more selective, because he is dealing only with the singular date as such. And as you probably know, any *Date Painting* that isn't completed on the date in question, for whatever reason, is subsequently destroyed. So for many dates there are no pictures.

In Darboven's work, she is usually dealing with a century, that is, the unit of time that we as human beings can more or less experience and relate to. It is immaterial whether it is the 1900s, the 1800s, or the 1700s—the first two digits are generally omitted. She calculates the century *an sich*. The date 01.01.00 can be in 1900, in 2000, or in 1600—in this context it makes no difference. What matters to her is saying: "I am surveying the century as a whole." The structures that arise in the course of her calculations are what interest her. And the visual

possibilities that she has discovered as well.

Darboven formulated these in an early work, *Sechs Bücher über 1968* (1968, *Six Books about 1968*), in which the year 1968 is presented in six different ways. A film version was derived from it, that is to say, six films were projected at the same time. That way the message becomes even clearer: in each case you have the same material, the year 1968, but each time it is structured in a different way, and so you obtain completely different progressions, completely different visual phenomena. That, I think, is what interests her.

And then, many years later, by way of a detour, so to speak, by way of music, she acquired the ability to structure time in yet another way, namely, musically. (Perhaps I also ought to mention that she was raised as a musician, and that music has always interested her greatly.)

SO: Darboven has said, "My work ends in music." Do you see that too? Do you think she will continue this way?

GDV: Perhaps that is putting it a bit strongly, a little like Mallarmé's "everything in the world is there so that it can end up in a book." Very nicely put, and for a writer very plausible, but surely

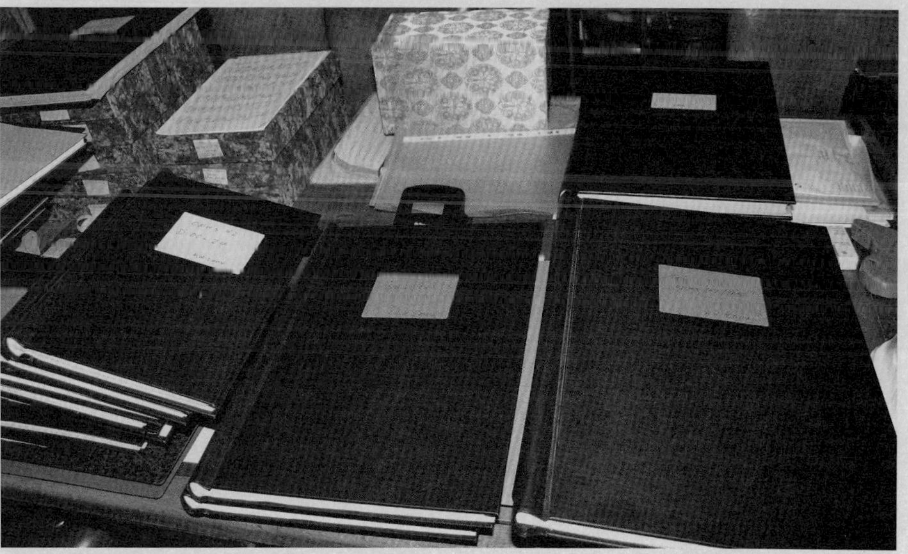

MUSICAL NOTEBOOKS IN DARBOVEN'S HOME, 2004

exaggerated. Artists tend to overstate things a bit to emphasize what they are all about. But I do think that music as structured time truly interests Darboven greatly, and that for some years now it has been more exciting to her than her fine art. At the moment, at least, she is producing musical works exclusively. In any case, music is a very, very, important part of her creative life. More than for any other fine artist I know.

SO: That's a good comment to end with.

Notes

1   See Hanne Darboven, *Aufzeichnung: Kosmos >85<* (1985–86), in *Hanne Darboven. "Histoire de la Culture, 1880–1983,"* exh. cat., ed. Suzanne Pagé (Paris: Musée de l'art moderne de la Ville de Paris, 1986), pp. 13f. The pages describing her musical system were reprinted in Hanne Darboven, "Catalogue for the concert . . . on April 28, 1999, in Berlin, and May 4, 1999, in Bonn," ed. Ingrid Buschmann, Gabriele Knapstein, and Gerd de Vries (Berlin: Nationalgalerie im Hamburger Bahnhof—Museum für Gegenwart; Bonn: Kunst-und Ausstellungshalle der Bundesrepublik Deutschland, 1999), p. 56. Darboven's *Kulturgeschichte* (*History of Culture*) deals with the years 1880–1983 and was created between 1980 and 1983.

2   For further information on the various methods of calculating the century and their transposition into musical notes, see Darboven, "Catalogue for the concert . . . on April 28, 1999, in Berlin, and May 4, 1999, in Bonn," p. 57.

3   In Marx's essay, "'A Section of Something That Has Eternally Begun and Will Continue to Sound Forever': Hanne Darboven's Time Music," which appears on pages 69–73 of this catalogue, he makes a precise accounting of the method he uses to derive a proper score from the "Darboven score."

4   *Cultural History 1880–1983, World Views 00–99* (1975–80), *World Theater ›79‹* (1979), *Evolution ›86‹* (1986), *Existence 66–88* (1989).

5   See also Cage's *Études Australes* for piano, which are based on star charts of the Australian sky.

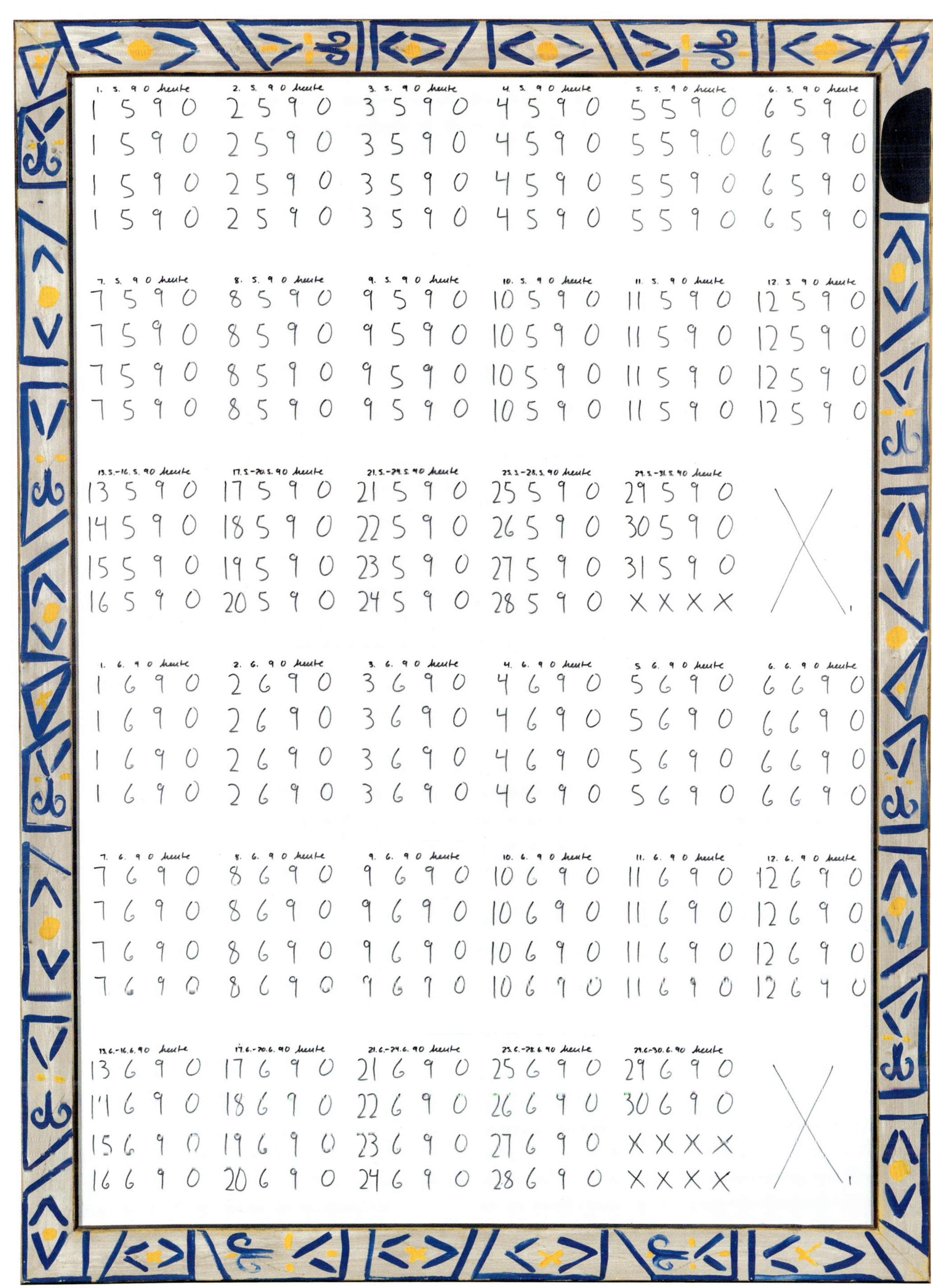

Framed text panels, from Hanne Darboven, *Hommage à Picasso*, 1995–2006.
Felt-tip pen on parchment paper in painted wooden frames, 196.5 × 144 cm each panel, 36 sheets per panel, 30 × 21 cm each sheet.

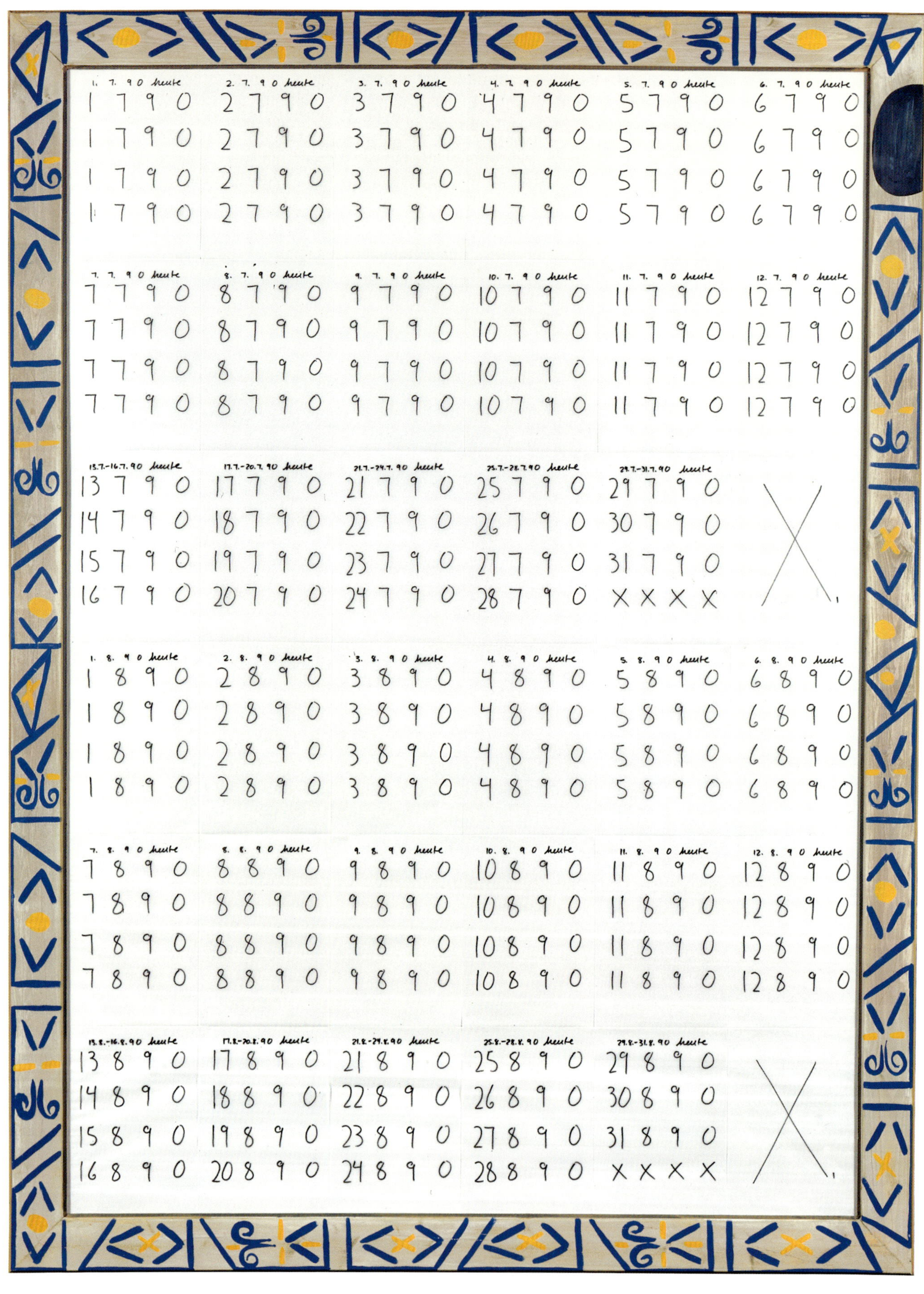

1. 7. 90 heute   2. 7. 90 heute   3. 7. 90 heute   4. 7. 90 heute   5. 7. 90 heute   6. 7. 90 heute
1 7 9 0   2 7 9 0   3 7 9 0   4 7 9 0   5 7 9 0   6 7 9 0
1 7 9 0   2 7 9 0   3 7 9 0   4 7 9 0   5 7 9 0   6 7 9 0
1 7 9 0   2 7 9 0   3 7 9 0   4 7 9 0   5 7 9 0   6 7 9 0
1 7 9 0   2 7 9 0   3 7 9 0   4 7 9 0   5 7 9 0   6 7 9 0
7. 7. 90 heute   8. 7. 90 heute   9. 7. 90 heute   10. 7. 90 heute   11. 7. 90 heute   12. 7. 90 heute
7 7 9 0   8 7 9 0   9 7 9 0   10 7 9 0   11 7 9 0   12 7 9 0
7 7 9 0   8 7 9 0   9 7 9 0   10 7 9 0   11 7 9 0   12 7 9 0
7 7 9 0   8 7 9 0   9 7 9 0   10 7 9 0   11 7 9 0   12 7 9 0
7 7 9 0   8 7 9 0   9 7 9 0   10 7 9 0   11 7 9 0   12 7 9 0
13.7.-16.7. 90 heute   17.7.-20.7. 90 heute   21.7.-24.7. 90 heute   25.7.-28.7. 90 heute   29.7.-31.7. 90 heute
13 7 9 0   17 7 9 0   21 7 9 0   25 7 9 0   29 7 9 0
14 7 9 0   18 7 9 0   22 7 9 0   26 7 9 0   30 7 9 0
15 7 9 0   19 7 9 0   23 7 9 0   27 7 9 0   31 7 9 0
16 7 9 0   20 7 9 0   24 7 9 0   28 7 9 0   X X X X
1. 8. 9 0 heute   2. 8. 90 heute   3. 8. 90 heute   4. 8. 90 heute   5. 8. 90 heute   6. 8. 90 heute
1 8 9 0   2 8 9 0   3 8 9 0   4 8 9 0   5 8 9 0   6 8 9 0
1 8 9 0   2 8 9 0   3 8 9 0   4 8 9 0   5 8 9 0   6 8 9 0
1 8 9 0   2 8 9 0   3 8 9 0   4 8 9 0   5 8 9 0   6 8 9 0
1 8 9 0   2 8 9 0   3 8 9 0   4 8 9 0   5 8 9 0   6 8 9 0
7. 8. 9 0 heute   8. 8. 9 0 heute   9. 8. 9 0 heute   10. 8. 9 0 heute   11. 8. 9 0 heute   12. 8. 9 0 heute
7 8 9 0   8 8 9 0   9 8 9 0   10 8 9 0   11 8 9 0   12 8 9 0
7 8 9 0   8 8 9 0   9 8 9 0   10 8 9 0   11 8 9 0   12 8 9 0
7 8 9 0   8 8 9 0   9 8 9 0   10 8 9 0   11 8 9 0   12 8 9 0
7 8 9 0   8 8 9 0   9 8 9 0   10 8 9 0   11 8 9 0   12 8 9 0
13.8.-16.8. 90 heute   17.8.-20.8. 90 heute   21.8.-24.8. 90 heute   25.8.-28.8. 90 heute   29.8.-31.8. 90 heute
13 8 9 0   17 8 9 0   21 8 9 0   25 8 9 0   29 8 9 0
14 8 9 0   18 8 9 0   22 8 9 0   26 8 9 0   30 8 9 0
15 8 9 0   19 8 9 0   23 8 9 0   27 8 9 0   31 8 9 0
16 8 9 0   20 8 9 0   24 8 9 0   28 8 9 0   X X X X

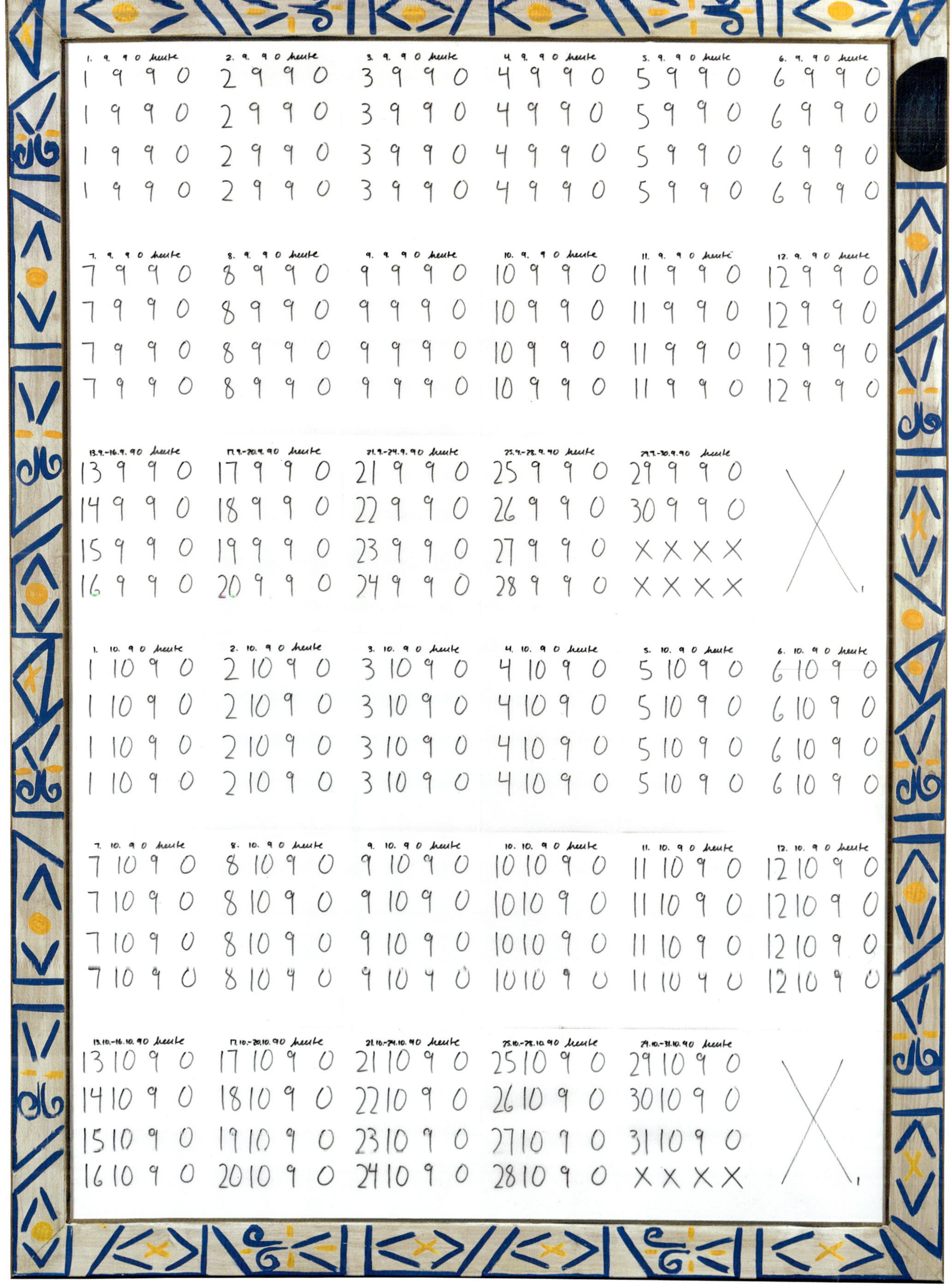

1. 9. 90 heute   2. 9. 90 heute   3. 9. 90 heute   4. 9. 90 heute   5. 9. 90 heute   6. 9. 90 heute
1 9 9 0   2 9 9 0   3 9 9 0   4 9 9 0   5 9 9 0   6 9 9 0
1 9 9 0   2 9 9 0   3 9 9 0   4 9 9 0   5 9 9 0   6 9 9 0
1 9 9 0   2 9 9 0   3 9 9 0   4 9 9 0   5 9 9 0   6 9 9 0
1 9 9 0   2 9 9 0   3 9 9 0   4 9 9 0   5 9 9 0   6 9 9 0

7. 9. 90 heute   8. 9. 90 heute   9. 9. 90 heute   10. 9. 90 heute   11. 9. 90 heute   12. 9. 90 heute
7 9 9 0   8 9 9 0   9 9 9 0   10 9 9 0   11 9 9 0   12 9 9 0
7 9 9 0   8 9 9 0   9 9 9 0   10 9 9 0   11 9 9 0   12 9 9 0
7 9 9 0   8 9 9 0   9 9 9 0   10 9 9 0   11 9 9 0   12 9 9 0
7 9 9 0   8 9 9 0   9 9 9 0   10 9 9 0   11 9 9 0   12 9 9 0

13.9.–16.9. 90 heute   17.9.–20.9. 90 heute   21.9.–24.9. 90 heute   25.9.–28.9. 90 heute   29.9.–30.9. 90 heute
13 9 9 0   17 9 9 0   21 9 9 0   25 9 9 0   29 9 9 0
14 9 9 0   18 9 9 0   22 9 9 0   26 9 9 0   30 9 9 0
15 9 9 0   19 9 9 0   23 9 9 0   27 9 9 0   X X X X
16 9 9 0   20 9 9 0   24 9 9 0   28 9 9 0   X X X X

1. 10. 90 heute   2. 10. 90 heute   3. 10. 90 heute   4. 10. 90 heute   5. 10. 90 heute   6. 10. 90 heute
1 10 9 0   2 10 9 0   3 10 9 0   4 10 9 0   5 10 9 0   6 10 9 0
1 10 9 0   2 10 9 0   3 10 9 0   4 10 9 0   5 10 9 0   6 10 9 0
1 10 9 0   2 10 9 0   3 10 9 0   4 10 9 0   5 10 9 0   6 10 9 0
1 10 9 0   2 10 9 0   3 10 9 0   4 10 9 0   5 10 9 0   6 10 9 0

7. 10. 90 heute   8. 10. 90 heute   9. 10. 90 heute   10. 10. 90 heute   11. 10. 90 heute   12. 10. 90 heute
7 10 9 0   8 10 9 0   9 10 9 0   10 10 9 0   11 10 9 0   12 10 9 0
7 10 9 0   8 10 9 0   9 10 9 0   10 10 9 0   11 10 9 0   12 10 9 0
7 10 9 0   8 10 9 0   9 10 9 0   10 10 9 0   11 10 9 0   12 10 9 0
7 10 9 0   8 10 9 0   9 10 9 0   10 10 9 0   11 10 9 0   12 10 9 0

13.10.–16.10. 90 heute   17.10.–20.10. 90 heute   21.10.–24.10. 90 heute   25.10.–28.10. 90 heute   29.10.–31.10. 90 heute
13 10 9 0   17 10 9 0   21 10 9 0   25 10 9 0   29 10 9 0
14 10 9 0   18 10 9 0   22 10 9 0   26 10 9 0   30 10 9 0
15 10 9 0   19 10 9 0   23 10 9 0   27 10 9 0   31 10 9 0
16 10 9 0   20 10 9 0   24 10 9 0   28 10 9 0   X X X X

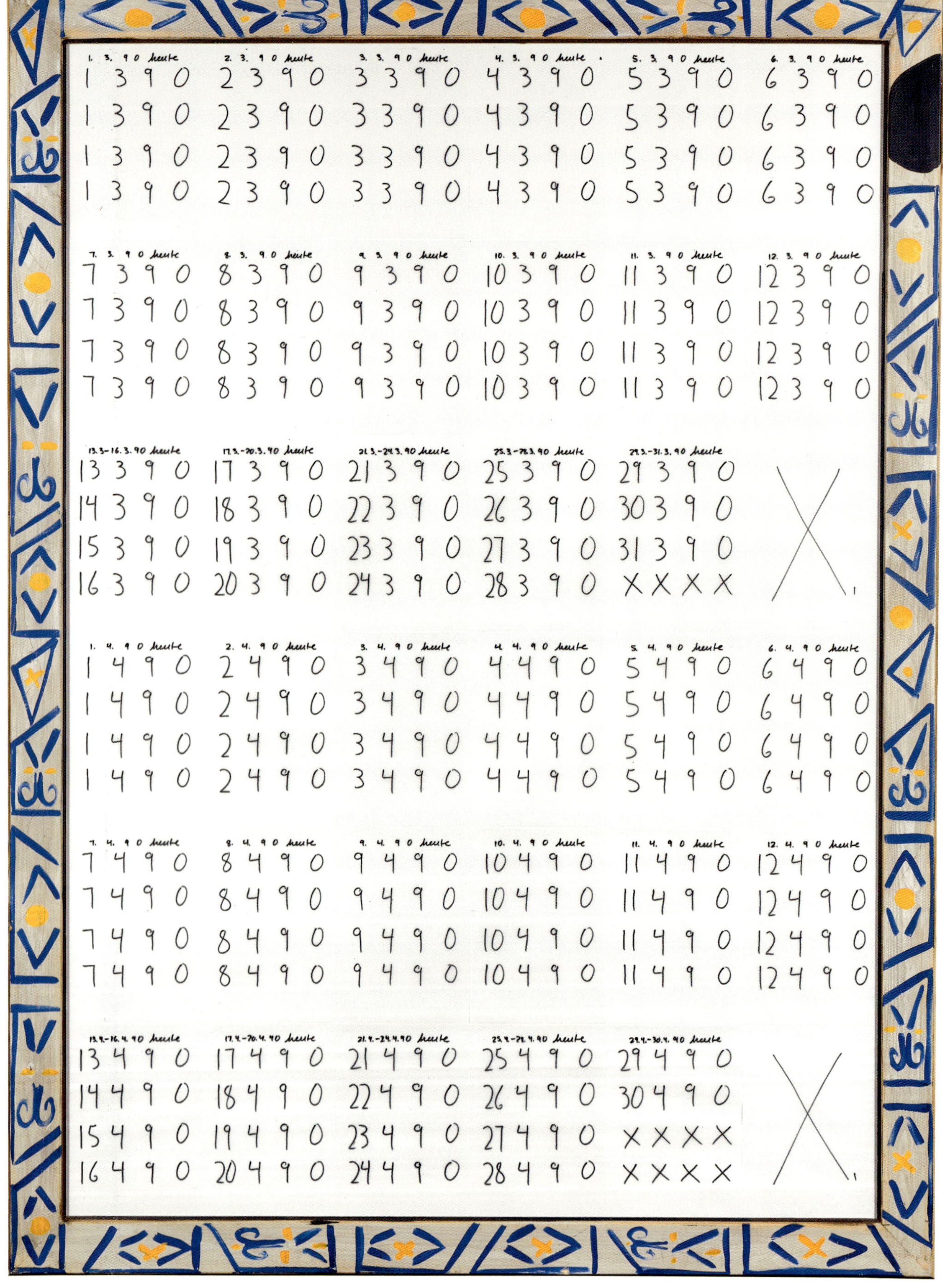

1. 3. 90 heute   2. 3. 90 heute   3. 3. 90 heute   4. 3. 90 heute   5. 3. 90 heute   6. 3. 90 heute
7. 3. 90 heute   8. 3. 90 heute   9. 3. 90 heute   10. 3. 90 heute   11. 3. 90 heute   12. 3. 90 heute
13.3.-16.3.90 heute   17.3.-20.3.90 heute   21.3.-24.3.90 heute   25.3.-28.3.90 heute   29.3.-31.3.90 heute
1. 4. 90 heute   2. 4. 90 heute   3. 4. 90 heute   4. 4. 90 heute   5. 4. 90 heute   6. 4. 90 heute
7. 4. 90 heute   8. 4. 90 heute   9. 4. 90 heute   10. 4. 90 heute   11. 4. 90 heute   12. 4. 90 heute
13.4.-16.4.90 heute   17.4.-20.4.90 heute   21.4.-24.4.90 heute   25.4.-28.4.90 heute   29.4.-30.4.90 heute

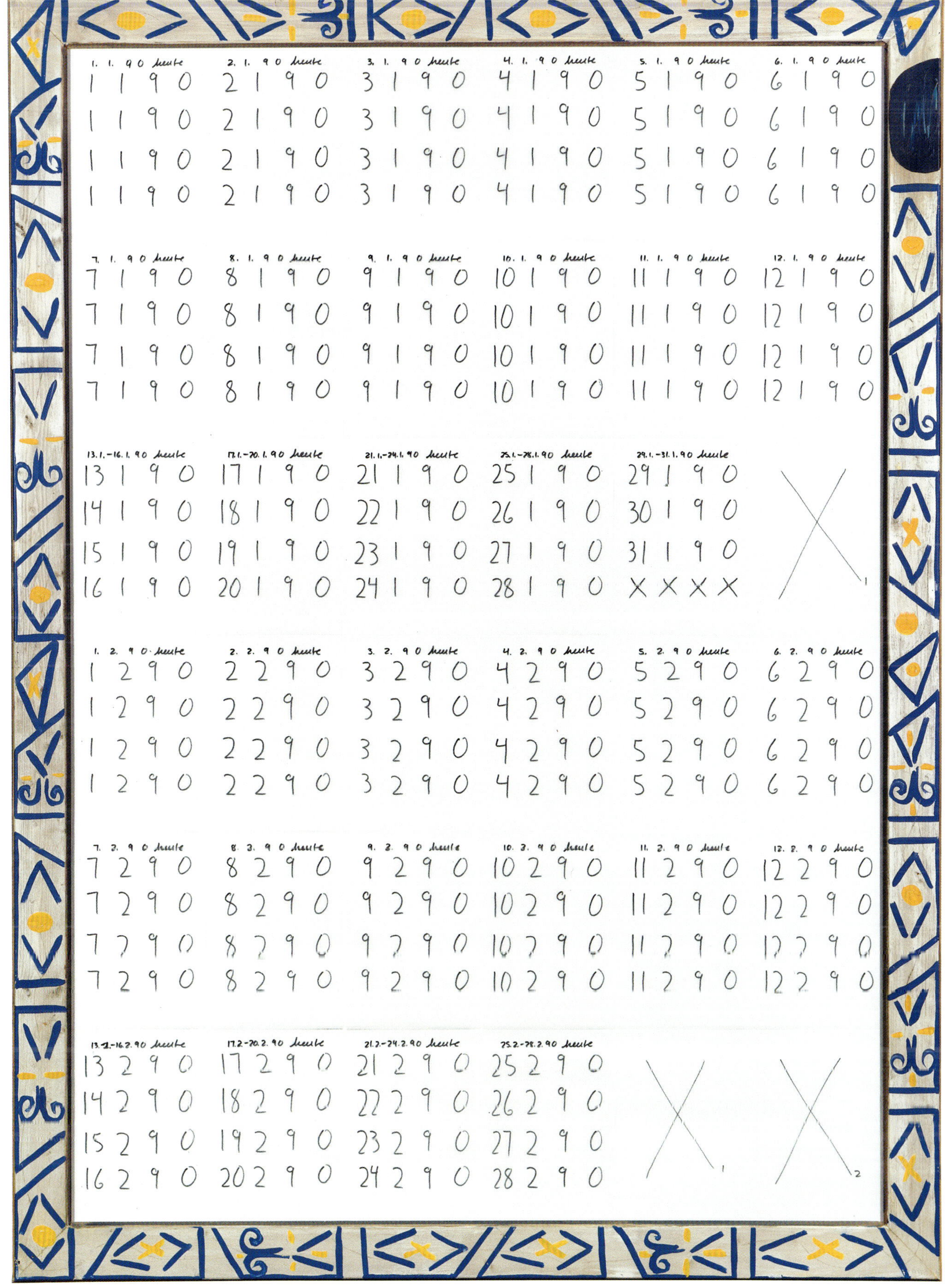

1. 1. 9 0 heute   2. 1. 9 0 heute   3. 1. 9 0 heute   4. 1. 9 0 heute   5. 1. 9 0 heute   6. 1. 9 0 heute
1 1 9 0   2 1 9 0   3 1 9 0   4 1 9 0   5 1 9 0   6 1 9 0
1 1 9 0   2 1 9 0   3 1 9 0   4 1 9 0   5 1 9 0   6 1 9 0
1 1 9 0   2 1 9 0   3 1 9 0   4 1 9 0   5 1 9 0   6 1 9 0
1 1 9 0   2 1 9 0   3 1 9 0   4 1 9 0   5 1 9 0   6 1 9 0

7. 1. 9 0 heute   8. 1. 9 0 heute   9. 1. 9 0 heute   10. 1. 9 0 heute   11. 1. 9 0 heute   12. 1. 9 0 heute
7 1 9 0   8 1 9 0   9 1 9 0   10 1 9 0   11 1 9 0   12 1 9 0
7 1 9 0   8 1 9 0   9 1 9 0   10 1 9 0   11 1 9 0   12 1 9 0
7 1 9 0   8 1 9 0   9 1 9 0   10 1 9 0   11 1 9 0   12 1 9 0
7 1 9 0   8 1 9 0   9 1 9 0   10 1 9 0   11 1 9 0   12 1 9 0

13.1.-16.1.90 heute   17.1.-20.1.90 heute   21.1.-24.1.90 heute   25.1.-28.1.90 heute   29.1.-31.1.90 heute
13 1 9 0   17 1 9 0   21 1 9 0   25 1 9 0   29 1 9 0
14 1 9 0   18 1 9 0   22 1 9 0   26 1 9 0   30 1 9 0
15 1 9 0   19 1 9 0   23 1 9 0   27 1 9 0   31 1 9 0
16 1 9 0   20 1 9 0   24 1 9 0   28 1 9 0   X X X

1. 2. 9 0 heute   2. 2. 9 0 heute   3. 2. 9 0 heute   4. 2. 9 0 heute   5. 2. 9 0 heute   6. 2. 9 0 heute
1 2 9 0   2 2 9 0   3 2 9 0   4 2 9 0   5 2 9 0   6 2 9 0
1 2 9 0   2 2 9 0   3 2 9 0   4 2 9 0   5 2 9 0   6 2 9 0
1 2 9 0   2 2 9 0   3 2 9 0   4 2 9 0   5 2 9 0   6 2 9 0
1 2 9 0   2 2 9 0   3 2 9 0   4 2 9 0   5 2 9 0   6 2 9 0

7. 2. 9 0 heute   8. 2. 9 0 heute   9. 2. 9 0 heute   10. 2. 9 0 heute   11. 2. 9 0 heute   12. 2. 9 0 heute
7 2 9 0   8 2 9 0   9 2 9 0   10 2 9 0   11 2 9 0   12 2 9 0
7 2 9 0   8 2 9 0   9 2 9 0   10 2 9 0   11 2 9 0   12 2 9 0
7 2 9 0   8 2 9 0   9 2 9 0   10 2 9 0   11 2 9 0   12 2 9 0
7 2 9 0   8 2 9 0   9 2 9 0   10 2 9 0   11 2 9 0   12 2 9 0

13.2.-16.2.90 heute   17.2.-20.2.90 heute   21.2.-24.2.90 heute   25.2.-28.2.90 heute
13 2 9 0   17 2 9 0   21 2 9 0   25 2 9 0
14 2 9 0   18 2 9 0   22 2 9 0   26 2 9 0
15 2 9 0   19 2 9 0   23 2 9 0   27 2 9 0
16 2 9 0   20 2 9 0   24 2 9 0   28 2 9 0

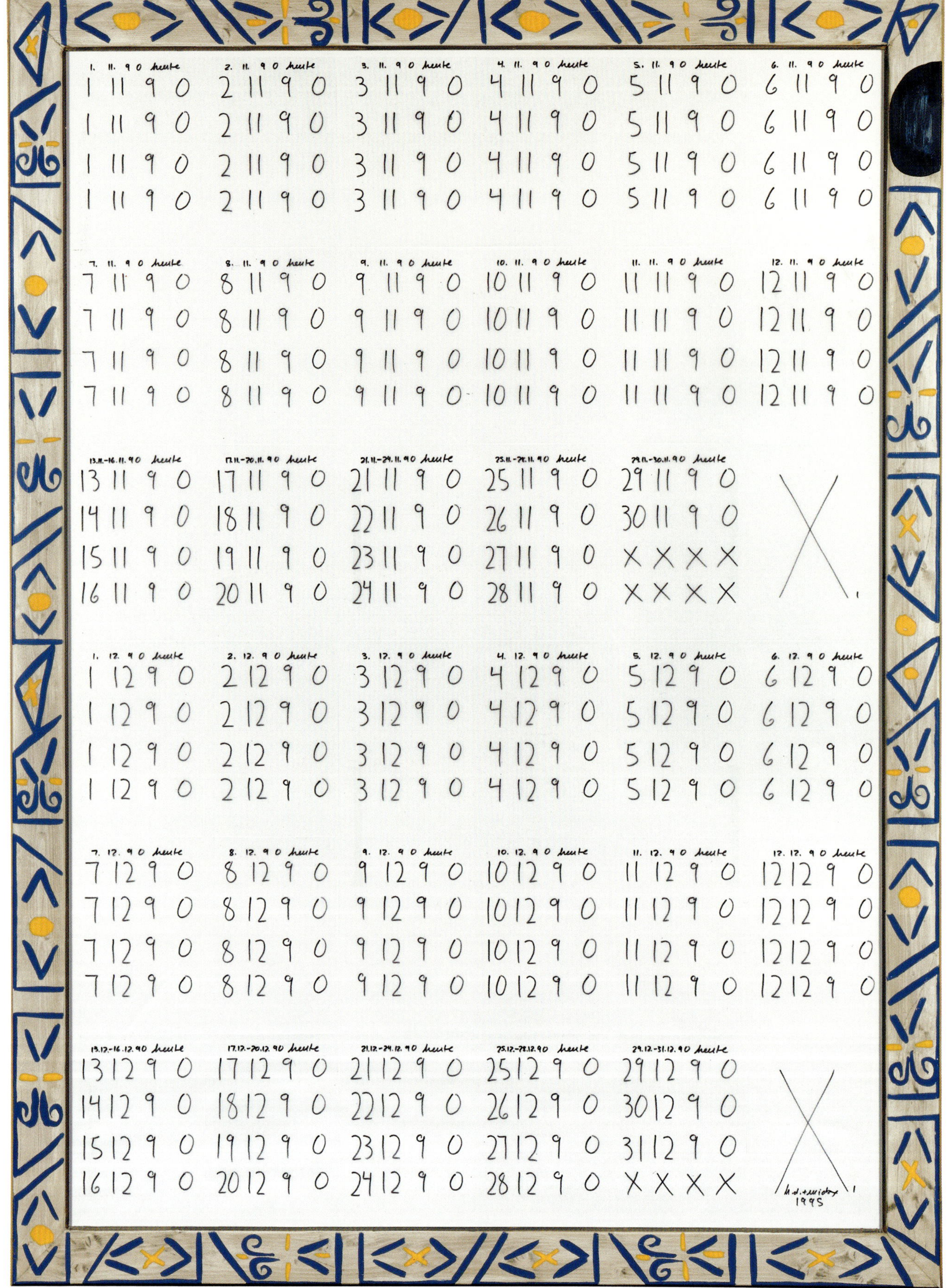

"A Section of Something That Has Eternally Begun and Will Continue to Sound Forever": Hanne Darboven's Time Music

Wolfgang Marx[1]

MUSIC DOES NOT EXIST ALL AT ONCE LIKE A PAINTING BUT IT UNROLLS ITSELF. NEVERTHELESS, WE MUST CONSIDER IT IN THE TERMS OF A PAINTING AS SOMETHING THAT EXISTS ALL AT ONCE. IN OTHER WORDS, TIME IS OUR MUSICAL CANVAS, NOT THE NOTES AND TIMBRES OF THE ORCHESTRA OR THE MELODIES AND TUNES OR THE TONAL FORMS HANDED DOWN TO US BY THE GREAT MASTERS.[2]

—GEORGE ANTHEIL

Hanne Darboven's music represents time. This seems to be a platitude, given that music is defined as an art of time (as indicated by the American composer's George Antheil's remark quoted above); any piece of music shapes the flow of time in a special and unique manner. Yet in the case of Darboven this is to be understood in a more literal way: She creates musical motifs or formulas based on dates, juxtaposing them simultaneously as well as in succession. She has made different constellations of every day of the twentieth century from 1 January 1900 until 31 December 1999. Thus all identical days of the different years (for example, all 1 Januaries) or all identical days of different months (4 January, 4 February, etc.) can be juxtaposed. Her music is not just shaping our perception of the time it takes to perform it; it is representing time quite literally.

In the case of Opus 60 each day is represented in music by a succession of ten notes. The note "D" signifies 0, "E" stands for 1, "F" for 2, and so forth, until an octave higher "D'" signifies 7, "E'" 8, and "F'" 9. The date 13 February 1990 is spelled 13020900 and is represented by the melodic formula E-G-D-F-D-F'-D-D.

The numerical representation of the date is always completed by the cross sum of its numbers; in this case, it is 24 (13+2+9). Hence the entire "day pattern" is 1302090024 (E-G-D-F-D-F'-D-D-F-A'). These notes, as represented in Darboven's idiosyncratic notation, can be seen in the first line of the figure below.[3]

This way of transforming numbers into notes is of course to some extent arbitrary; one could choose other notes, make use of the chromatic scales of semitones instead of diatonic ones, or count downward instead of upward (as the ancient Greeks did, for instance). The solution chosen here is one based on our cultural heritage—other cultures like the ancient Babylonians would have formed these patterns in a completely different way, as their numbering system was based on twelve rather than ten numerals (a fact still reflected in our way of measuring time). In the Middle Ages, when the treble (or, G) clef was hardly ever used

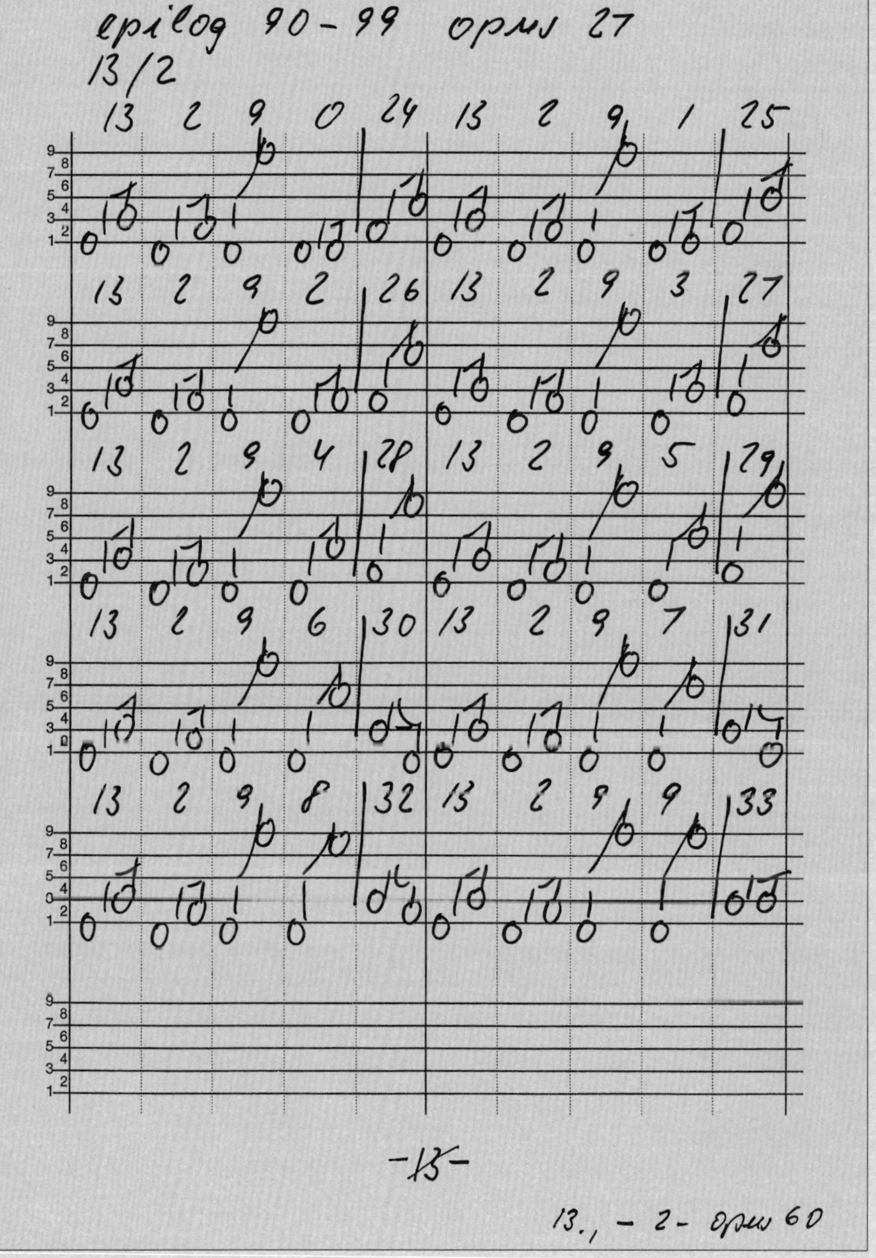

HANNE DARBOVEN, AUTOGRAPH OF OPUS 60, SECTION 13, SECOND PART (ALSO USED IN OPUS 27)

while C clefs were quite common, another note instead of "D" would have served as root of the scale. Yet any of these "codes" is as arbitrary as the one Darboven has developed. What is important is only that the chosen way is pursued consistently.

A listener unfamiliar with this code is hardly able to decipher the dates behind the music. In the case of multipart pieces like Opus 60 (it has 120 parts), even the knowledgeable listener will be at a loss, as too many parts are played simultaneously—or, in other words, as too many days pass at the same time. This can be compared to the French composer Olivier Messiaen's use of the so-called *langage communicable* in his organ cycle *Méditations sur le Mystére de la Sainte Trinité* (1969). In this "communicable language," letters are represented by combinations of certain pitches, note values, dynamic levels, and modes of attack. Messiaen used this language to "translate" a text by Saint Thomas Aquinas into music. Without consulting the score, few listeners will be able to "understand" this text. Yet more important than this understanding is the expressive quality of the music. In the case of Darboven, it arises from juxtapositions of day patterns. Their interaction results in a series of sections that have no obvious beginning nor ending. A similar effect can be found in compositions by the Hungarian composer György Ligeti from the 1960s. For instance, Ligeti described his composition *Lontano* (1967) as follows:

IT IS MUSIC THAT GIVES THE IMPRESSION THAT IT COULD STREAM ON CONTINUOUSLY, AS IF IT HAD NO BEGINNING AND NO END; WHAT WE HEAR IS ACTUALLY A SECTION OF SOMETHING THAT HAS ETERNALLY BEGUN AND WILL CONTINUE TO SOUND FOREVER.[4]

Ligeti achieves this effect by writing a large number of contrapuntal lines, which together create an impression of stasis.

Darboven's patterns, on the other hand, are set in a homophonic manner; they always commence and end simultaneously. Yet as she is writing atonal music that uses neither cadential progressions nor complex internal formal structures, we perceive only the repetitive element of the patterns and do not realize straightaway when or why the piece will end. This seems fitting for a composition representing time: the piece ends when all the days of the century are "used," yet even a century is just a small fraction of the eternity of time: the music could conceivably continue ad infinitum.[5]

This infinite quality relates Darboven's music to another main current of contemporary music, namely, minimalist music, which works with short, gradually changing or shifting patterns. Apart from these patterns, in minimalist music there normally are not perceivable, major formal units or developments; hence this style has often been described as being without goals or direction. The musicologist Timothy A. Jackson, for instance, states:

THE FORM OF PIECES IN THE MINIMALIST STYLE IS PRIMARILY CONTINUOUS, OFTEN IN THE SHAPE OF AN UNBROKEN STREAM OF RHYTHMIC FIGURATION FLOWING FROM THE BEGINNING OF THE PIECE UNTIL IT ENDS. SOMETIMES THESE CONTINUOUS FORMS GROW GRADUALLY FROM SPARSE RHYTHMIC FRAMEWORKS OR WANE AFTER REACHING CLIMAXES. HOWEVER, IN ANY CASE DISTINCT DISJUNCT SECTIONS ARE GENERALLY NOT CHARACTERISTIC OF THE MINIMALIST STYLE.[6]

The patterns that appear in minimalist music are usually of a rhythmic rather than melodic nature. But for Darboven, of the three basic parameters of music (melody, harmony, rhythm), the first is obviously central, as her day patterns are of a melodic nature. The respective harmonic configuration is a result of the simultaneous juxtaposition of several day patterns, leading to unisons of just one pitch or chords of two, three, or ten notes. The succession of similar ten-note

patterns is perceived by the listener as the basic metric unit, yet there is no rhythm in the usual sense of the word, as all notes are of the same value in the original notation.

The transformation of Hanne Darboven's autograph into a composition to be performed requires certain interventions regarding the musical parameters not determined by the composer. To do this, I begin by transcribing her notation into our standard notation, in the process turning her eighth notes into quarter notes, since they are the basis of most time signatures. Then I have to consider two important questions: Is the music to be "rhythmicized," and if so, in what way? And how is a piece consisting of 120 parts to be orchestrated? Darboven does not indicate solutions to these questions; she only requests that the melodic structure of her patterns are not to be tampered with.

Opus 60 is made of 30 sections, each of which uses all 120 parts. Any part in any section is made of ten successive day patterns, each one differing in just two notes from the next one, as I will soon explain. Every section ends with a broken chord, which is not written down but intended by the composer, an ascending triad based on the last note of the respective part. As the triad can only make use of the ten notes of Darboven's scale, the use of chromatic notes is forbidden. Hence the result is a mixture of minor and major triads; in the case of the triad on "B," there is a diminished chord. Often several of these triads sound simultaneously, resulting in a cluster.

The fact that Darboven's "decatonic" scale commences on "D" and does not use chromatic notes could indicate to the listener that she writes in the Dorian church mode. Regardless of the structure of the successive chords and their often dissonant nature, one always recognizes "D" as the root of her scale. As a result, some earlier works by Darboven were arranged in such a way that a pseudo-tonal or pseudomodal sound was created. However, in the case of Opus 60, I have rejected this approach, as I think it would not do justice to the particular structure of this music. A different approach was to be found, an approach that on the one hand would preserve the special character of this music, while on the other hand deal with the aesthetic and pragmatic needs of musical presentation. Among the latter is, for instance, the need to grant brass players regular rests, as they cannot play large intervals for an hour or longer. If I wanted to use trumpets, trombones, or horns in the orchestra, they would need time to catch their breath, even if there are no specified rests in any of the 120 parts. The main aesthetic task was to find a way of enriching the repetitive elements by way of musical variants or even contrasts without sacrificing Darboven's basic structure.

My starting point when I began to work on the orchestration in earnest was the fact that if 120 instruments simultaneously play different day patterns, the same notes will often be played by several instruments at once. In any given chord of Opus 60 you can never hear more than the ten notes of Darboven's scale (although sometimes they are transposed an octave up or down); thus, in theory, ten instruments would be enough to represent all these chords (although limiting it to ten would mean sacrificing most of the melodic lines). Due to the high number of parts involved, single melodic lines can hardly be perceived; hence I decided not to set all sections for full orchestra (i.e., the tutti group), but to let it alternate with smaller groups of instruments.

In the figure to the right, you can see my transcription of the beginning of the thirteenth section of Opus 60 (the part seen in the figure on page 69 is represented by the top voice, set for double bass). A comparison of the different parts indicated here reveals that most of the notes are identical for each part—in fact, only the fourth and the tenth notes (representing the month and the last digit of the cross sum) seem to change. A look at all 120 parts would reveal that in fact the third and the ninth digit (representing the first digit of the month's number and the first digit of the cross sum) also change, although just occasionally. The first digit of the month uses only two numerals (0 and 1, the latter for only October, November, and December); the first digit of the cross sum is never more than 3. Thus the simultaneously sounding day patterns vary only in four out of ten digits/notes. So I had to create groupings of parts containing all the notes needed on the third, fourth, ninth, and tenth positions of the pattern. As I soon realized, the smallest number of parts that would allow me to achieve this was twelve. Hence I created five groups of twelve instruments each to be deployed at different points of the work. These five groups are woodwinds (four flutes, three oboes, three clarinets, two bassoons), brass (four trumpets, four French horns, three trombones, one tuba), saxophones (two soprano, four alto, four tenor, two bass), twelve solo violins, and twelve solo violoncellos. Whenever one of these groups is playing, we don't hear every single melodic line Darboven has written down, yet we do hear all the pitches she has notated. Thus the missing patterns are indirectly present.

Besides the groups of instruments mentioned above, the orchestra is made of an additional thirty-six violins, twelve violas, eight double basses, and four

TRANSCRIPTION OF OPUS 60, SECTION 13 (BEGINNING)

percussion instruments: triangle, tam-tam, drum, and timpani. The last four instruments do not of course play day patterns. Their parts are not played as melodic units, yet all their notes are always present in many other instruments' parts.

As mentioned before, in Darboven's musical compositions there is no large-scale musical form beyond the level of the day patterns, which is one of the reasons why it appears static, not moving in any particular direction. In order to transcend the repetitive patterns and join them with a large-scale formal structure, I decided to utilize techniques of different twentieth-century composers, namely, Arnold Schoenberg (or the Second Viennese School in general), John Cage, and Olivier Messiaen.

The formal structure I have opted for is that of a palindrome. Opus 60 gradually develops toward a climax at the center of the piece (sections 15 and 16) before declining in a way that mirrors the initial ascent. Scoring, tempo, rhythmic structure (also known as "modules," as will be explained later), and dynamics are identical in sections 1 and 30, 2 and 29, 3 and 28, and so forth, as the diagram to the right highlights.

The sections are orchestrated such that roughly every third section there is a tutti, while the groups of instruments mentioned above are used in between (in addition, the groups are supplemented by combinations of woodwinds and brass, woodwinds and strings, or all strings without woodwinds and brass). The central sections, 15 and 16, are the only ones to be played in fortissimo; they are also rhythmically the most complex. The overall impression of the piece is meant to be that of a music gradually emerging out of silence, reaching ever new heights in wavelike motions, climaxing in sections 15 and 16, and then gradually withdrawing.

The piece is a small segment of infinite time, which of course was running before the piece started and keeps going after it ends (as indicated in Ligeti's quote above).

Scoring, tempo, and rhythmic structure are mirrored symmetrically around the central axis of the piece; the same is not the case for the melodic structure of Darboven's notation—the tuba part in section 16 is not an exact "retrograde" (the original pattern version played backward) of the one in section 15, but instead,

NO.	SCORING	TEMPO	MODULE(S)	DYNAMICS
1/30	TUTTI	ANDANTE CON MOTO	A	pp
2/29	WOODWINDS, STRINGS	ADAGIO MA NON TROPPO	A, B, G	mp
3/28	VIOLONCELLI	LARGO	B	f
4/27	TUTTI	PRESTO	A, G	mf
5/26	SAXOPHONES	ALLEGRO	C	f
6/25	VIOLINS, VIOLONCELLI	ALLEGRO	B, E, F	mf
7/24	TUTTI	MODERATO	A, B, D	p
8/23	BRASS, WOODWINDS	FURIOSO	D	mf
9/22	SAXOPHONES	LENTO	E, F	mp
10/21	TUTTI	GRAVE	A, C	f
11/20	VIOLINS	ALLEGRO CON BRIO	A, D, E, F	mf
12/19	TUTTI	MODERATO	B, D, G	pp
13/18	WOODWINDS, STRINGS	PRESTO	E	mf
14/17	BRASS	CHORALE (MAESTOSO)	A	f
15/16	TUTTI	ANDANTE CON MOTO	A, B, D, E, F, G	ff

like all the sections that precede it, presents a new day pattern. Nevertheless there is a way of including the melodic structure in the palindrome as well: the parts can be transcribed in reverse. This technique was used extensively by Schoenberg and his pupils in the dodecaphonic style (in some pieces they not only used reversible twelve-tone rows but also mirrored the entire piece around a central axis). Alban Berg, Anton von Webern, Luigi Nono, and Humphrey Searle were among the composers writing these palindromic works.

In Opus 60, the parts transcribed in reverse are not identical to their "counter-parts" in the first half of the piece. Nevertheless, the overall impression is almost as if they were: the two ten-note clusters now sound not on the fourth and tenth but on the first and seventh notes of each pattern; the two- and three-note chords no longer occupy the third and ninth but the second and eighth positions.

The palindrome is in my opinion a very good concept when it comes to music representing time. This is indicated by the use of so-called "nonretrogradable rhythms" in the music of Messiaen. These rhythmic formulas are arranged in a palindromic pattern, so that their retrograde is identical with the original—hence they are "nonretrogradable." For Messiaen, a devout Catholic, this structure was meant to represent eternity, where there is no time and hence it is irrelevant whether it runs forward or backward. Darboven's representation of time is not based on religious convictions, yet she keeps reordering the dates again and again in her works. So, for instance, if all day patterns of the first days of a month are placed before the patterns of all seconds, 2 January would be played after 1

February (or 1 December, for that matter). So the order of time is manipulated and occasionally reversed in her work as well.

The structure of Darboven's music is determined to the extreme; the day patterns are ordered according to a rigid rule without exception. To loosen this structure, when rhythmicizing the piece I introduced an aleatoric element à la John Cage. I defined seven so-called "rhythmic modules," which are used separately or in combination in every section of Opus 60. If there are several modules "on offer,"

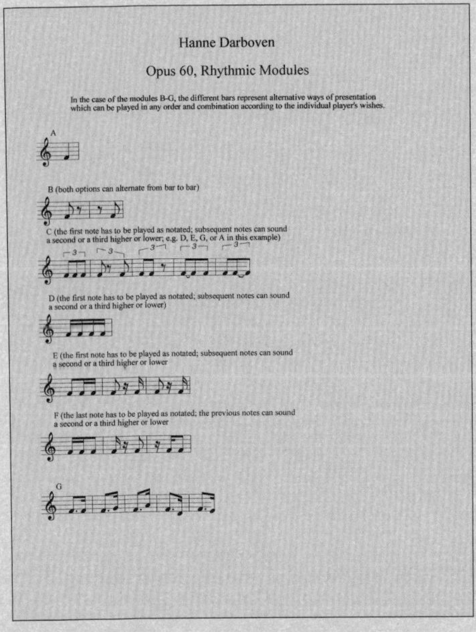

RHYTHMIC MODULES AS USED IN OPUS 60

every player can decide which one(s) to use and adjust his choice from note to note. This adds variety to the music, even though the notes are still notated in quarter notes (the modules are indicated on top of each section and apply to all parts). If a rhythmic module contains two or more notes, the first one has to be played on the indicated pitch, while the following ones can depart from it—yet only by step, using neighboring notes. This results in a spreading of clusters and a deviation from the regular alternation of unisons and clusters within the day patterns. The figure above presents the rhythmic modules.

One last remark regarding the expressive power of Hanne Darboven's works. This is not a primarily emotional or dramatic music; obviously, it is dominated by purely structural means. Similar to what Bach did in his *Art of the Fugue*, this is the transformation of theoretical-abstract ideas into music, and is not primarily based on concerns about performability (for instance, it does not indicate a scoring). Yet this does not mean that this music is not expressive. The American composer Christian Wolff has reflected on this paradox in an article on new and electronic music. His thoughts regarding an "objectified" music are addressing works by Cage, yet they can be applied to Darboven's compositions as well:

ONE FINDS A CONCERN FOR A KIND OF OBJECTIVITY . . . —SOUND COME INTO ITS OWN. THE "MUSIC" IS A RESULTANT EXISTING SIMPLY IN THE SOUNDS WE HEAR, GIVEN NO IMPULSE BY EXPRESSION OR SELF OR PERSONALITY. IT IS INDIFFERENT IN MOTIVE, ORIGINATING IN NO PSYCHOLOGY NOR IN DRAMATIC INTENTIONS, NOR IN LITERARY OR PICTORIAL PURPOSES. FOR AT LEAST SOME OF THESE COMPOSERS, THEN, THE FINAL INTENTION IS TO BE FREE OF ARTISTRY AND TASTE. BUT THIS NEED NOT MAKE THEIR WORK "ABSTRACT," FOR NOTHING, IN THE END, IS DENIED. IT IS SIMPLY THAT PERSONAL EXPRESSION, DRAMA, PSYCHOLOGY, AND THE LIKE ARE NOT PART OF THE COMPOSER'S INITIAL CALCULATION: THEY ARE AT BEST GRATUITOUS.[7]

In spite of its objective-determinist structure, Darboven's music has an astonishing expressive power, a fact I have tried to underline when arranging Opus 60 for orchestra.

Notes

1   Wolfgang Marx is a musicologist based at University College Dublin. Since 2002, he has worked with Hanne Darboven on the realization of her compositions, transcribing her musical scores into "standard" notation and arranging her pieces for performance.

2   George Antheil, letter to Nicolas Slonimsky in 1936, quoted in Daniel Albright, ed., *Modernism and Music: An Anthology of Sources* (Chicago: University of Chicago Press, 2004), p. 71.

3   The note "D" is used to signify 0, because it is placed straight under the lowest line of the staff. With this 0 as a starting point, the "F" on the top line comes to signify 9; thus the ten numerals fill the staff in a perfect way, without any need of introducing ledger lines. Darboven has developed her own manuscript paper, showing the numerals on the left-hand side next to each staff and separating the day patterns by a dividing vertical line in the center.

4   *György Ligeti in Conversation with Péter Várnai, Josef Häusler, Claude Samuel, and Himself* (London: Eulenburg Books, 1983), p. 84.

5   In Opus 60, Darboven has paid tribute to this fact by using only the last two digits of the respective year; thus the numbers can stand not just for the twentieth century but in fact for any century.

6   Timothy A. Jackson, "Minimalism: Aesthetic, Style, or Technique?," *The Musical Quarterly* 78, no. 4 (1994), p. 748. The American composer Christian Wolff has found this feature in works by other composers of the 1950s as well; among others he names are Henri Pousseur, Karlheinz Stockhausen, and John Cage: "Complexity tends to reach a point of neutralization: Continuous change results in a certain sameness. The music has a static character. It goes in no particular direction. . . . It is not a question of getting anywhere, of making progress, or having come from anywhere in particular." Quoted in John Cage, *Silence: Lectures and Writings* (Middletown, Conn.: Wesleyan University Press, 1968), p. 54.

7   Wolff, quoted in Cage, *Silence*, p. 68.

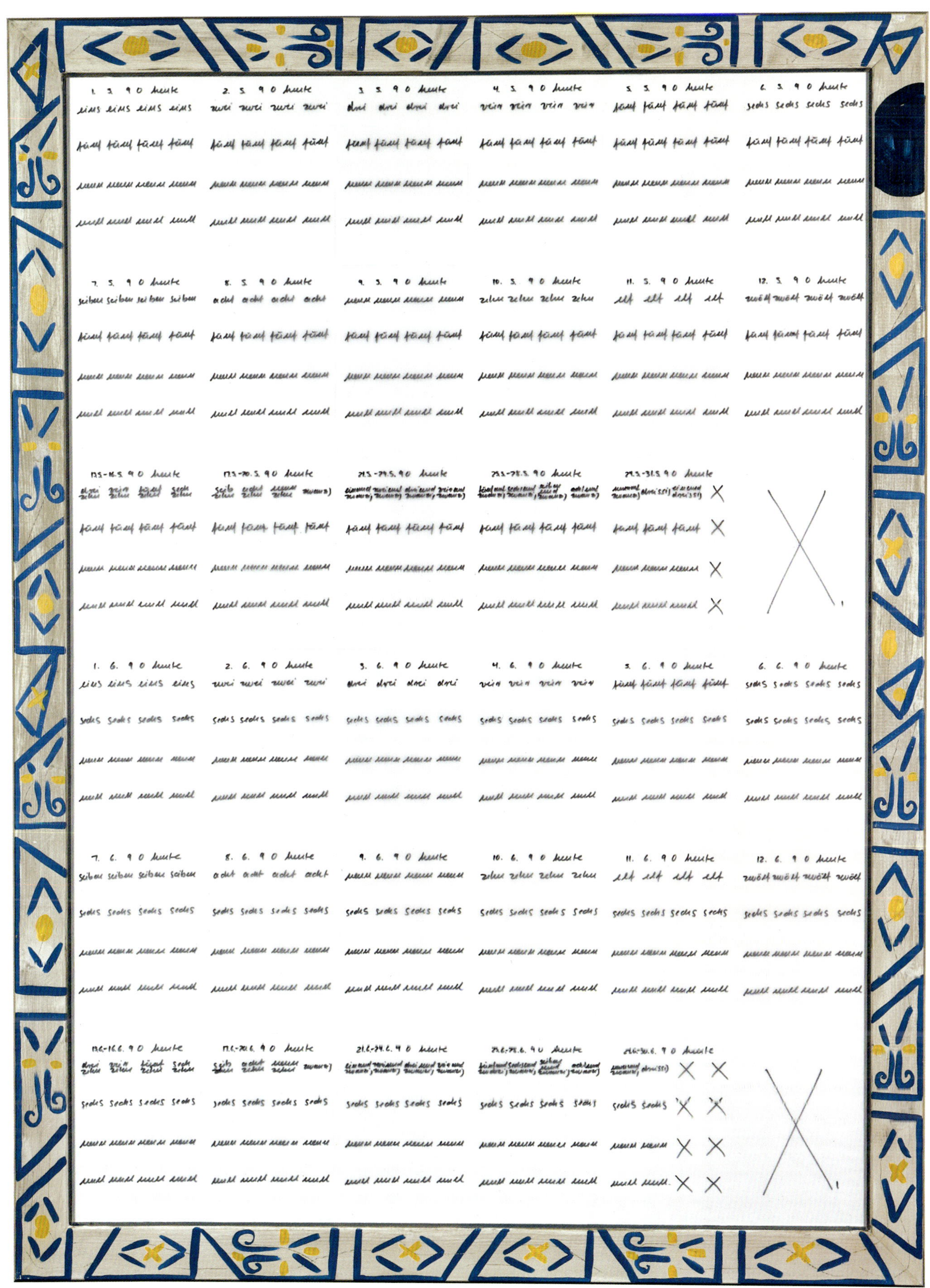

Framed text panels, from Hanne Darboven,
Hommage à Picasso, 1995–2006.
Felt-tip pen on parchment paper in painted
wooden frames, 196.5 × 144 cm each panel,
36 sheets per panel, 30 × 21 cm each sheet.

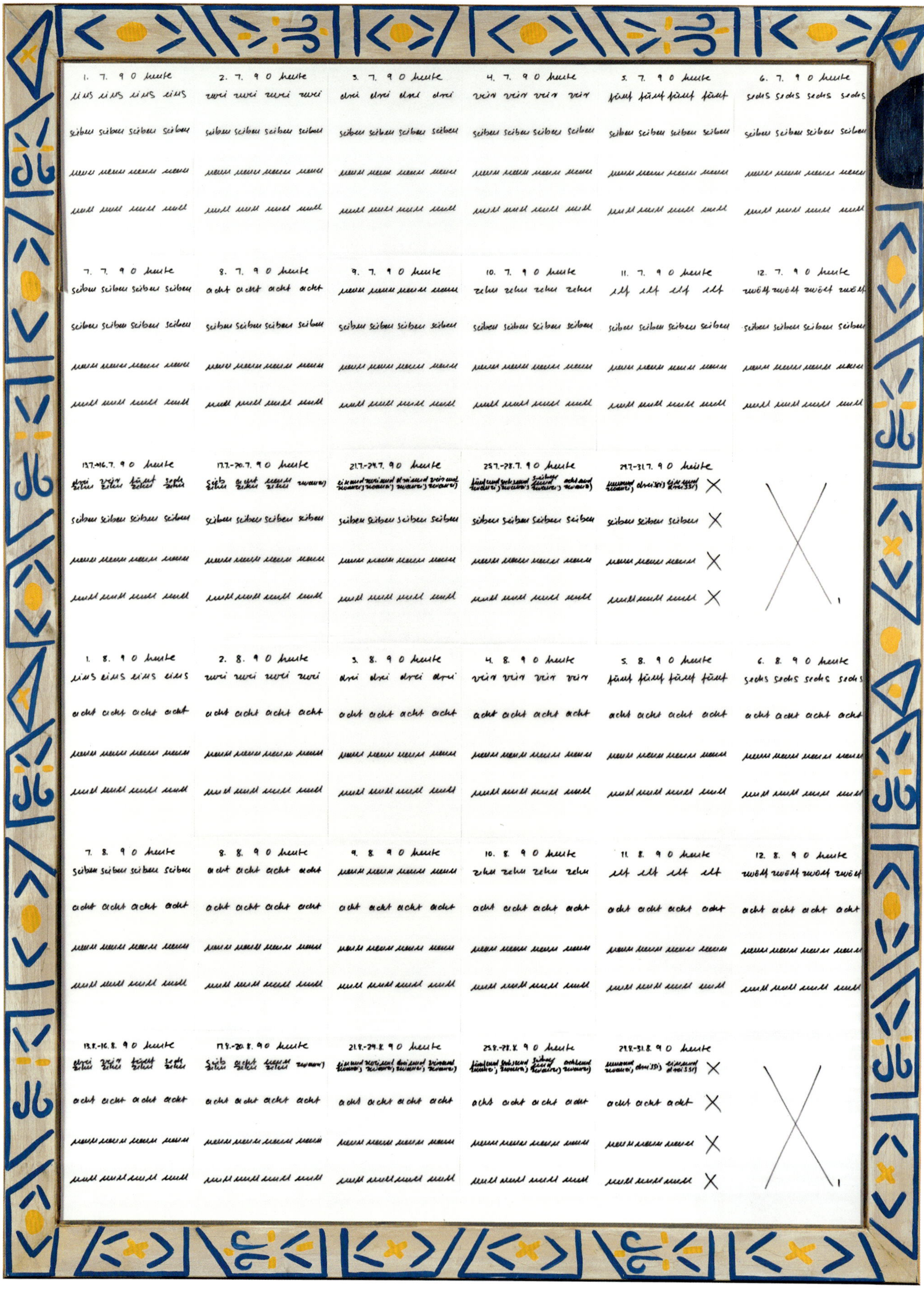

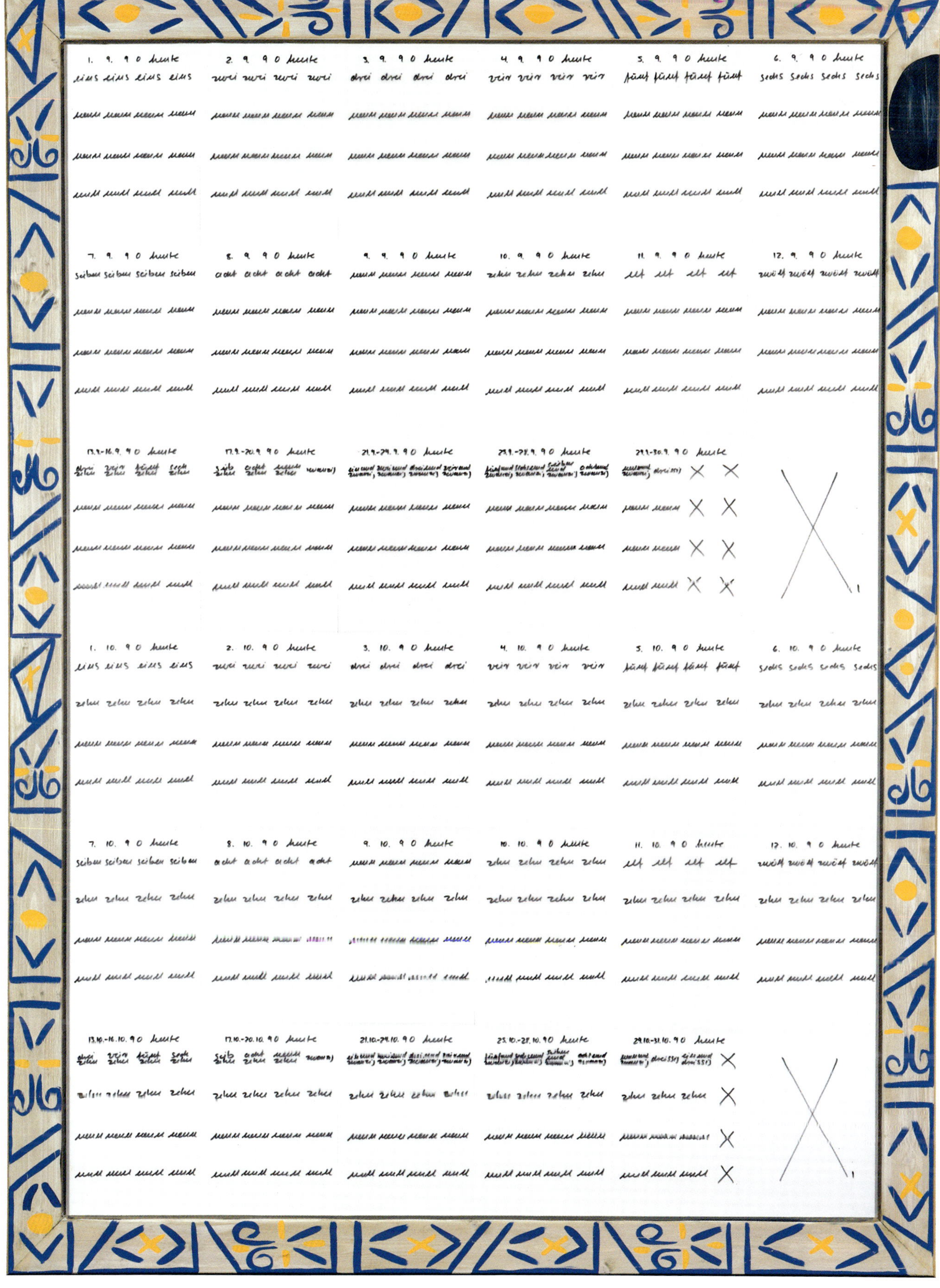

1. 9. 90 heute — eins eins eins eins
2. 9. 90 heute — zwei zwei zwei zwei
3. 9. 90 heute — drei drei drei drei
4. 9. 90 heute — vier vier vier vier
5. 9. 90 heute — fünf fünf fünf fünf
6. 9. 90 heute — sechs sechs sechs sechs
7. 9. 90 heute — sieben sieben sieben sieben
8. 9. 90 heute — acht acht acht acht
9. 9. 90 heute
10. 9. 90 heute — zehn zehn zehn zehn
11. 9. 90 heute — elf elf elf elf
12. 9. 90 heute — zwölf zwölf zwölf zwölf
13.9.–16.9. 90 heute
17.9.–20.9. 90 heute
21.9.–24.9. 90 heute
25.9.–28.9. 90 heute
29.9.–30.9. 90 heute
1. 10. 90 heute — eins eins eins eins
2. 10. 90 heute — zwei zwei zwei zwei
3. 10. 90 heute — drei drei drei drei
4. 10. 90 heute — vier vier vier vier
5. 10. 90 heute — fünf fünf fünf fünf
6. 10. 90 heute — sechs sechs sechs sechs
7. 10. 90 heute — sieben sieben sieben sieben
8. 10. 90 heute — acht acht acht acht
9. 10. 90 heute
10. 10. 90 heute — zehn zehn zehn zehn
11. 10. 90 heute — elf elf elf elf
12. 10. 90 heute — zwölf zwölf zwölf zwölf
13.10.–16.10. 90 heute
17.10.–20.10. 90 heute
21.10.–24.10. 90 heute
25.10.–28.10. 90 heute
29.10.–31.10. 90 heute

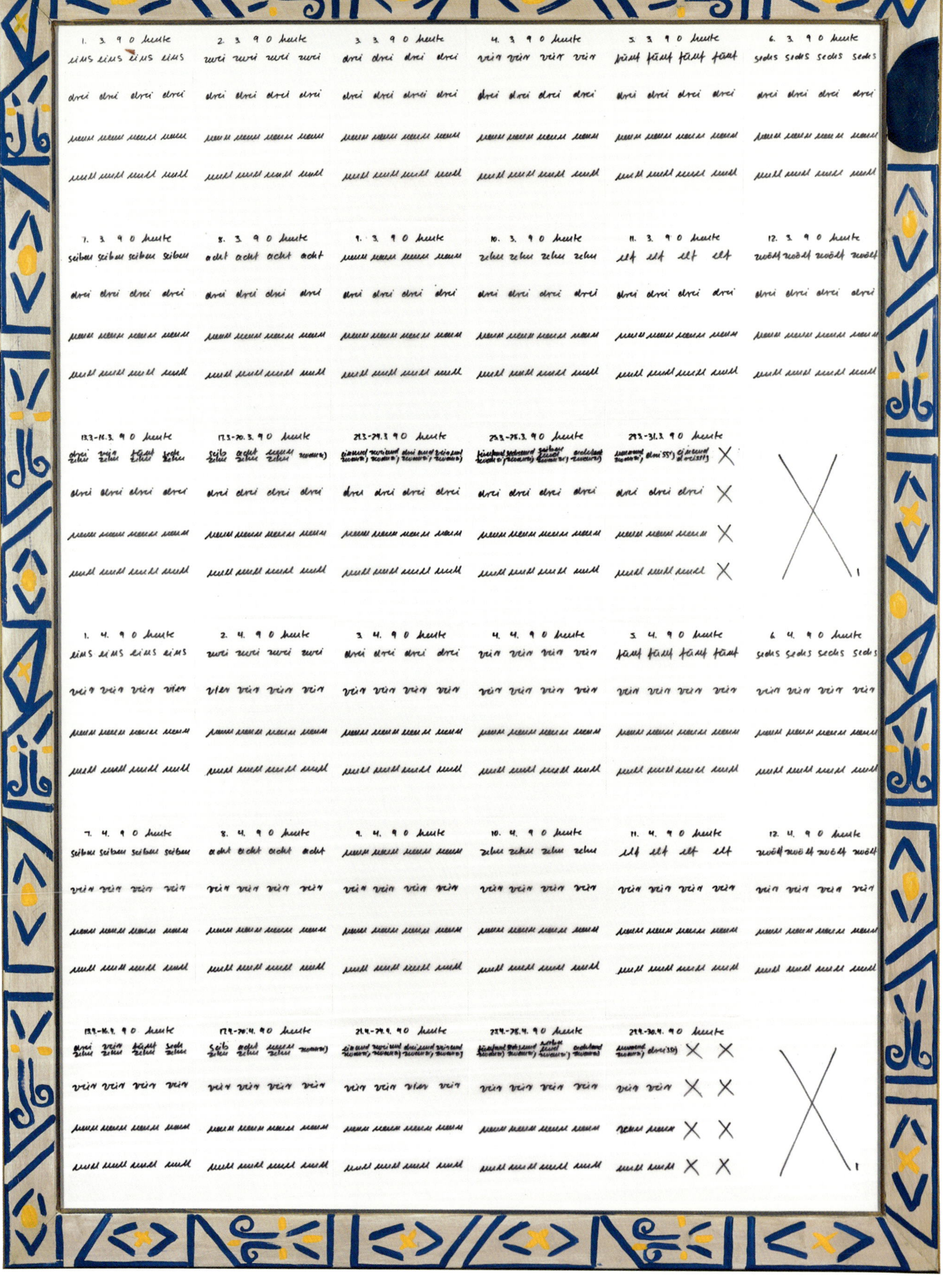

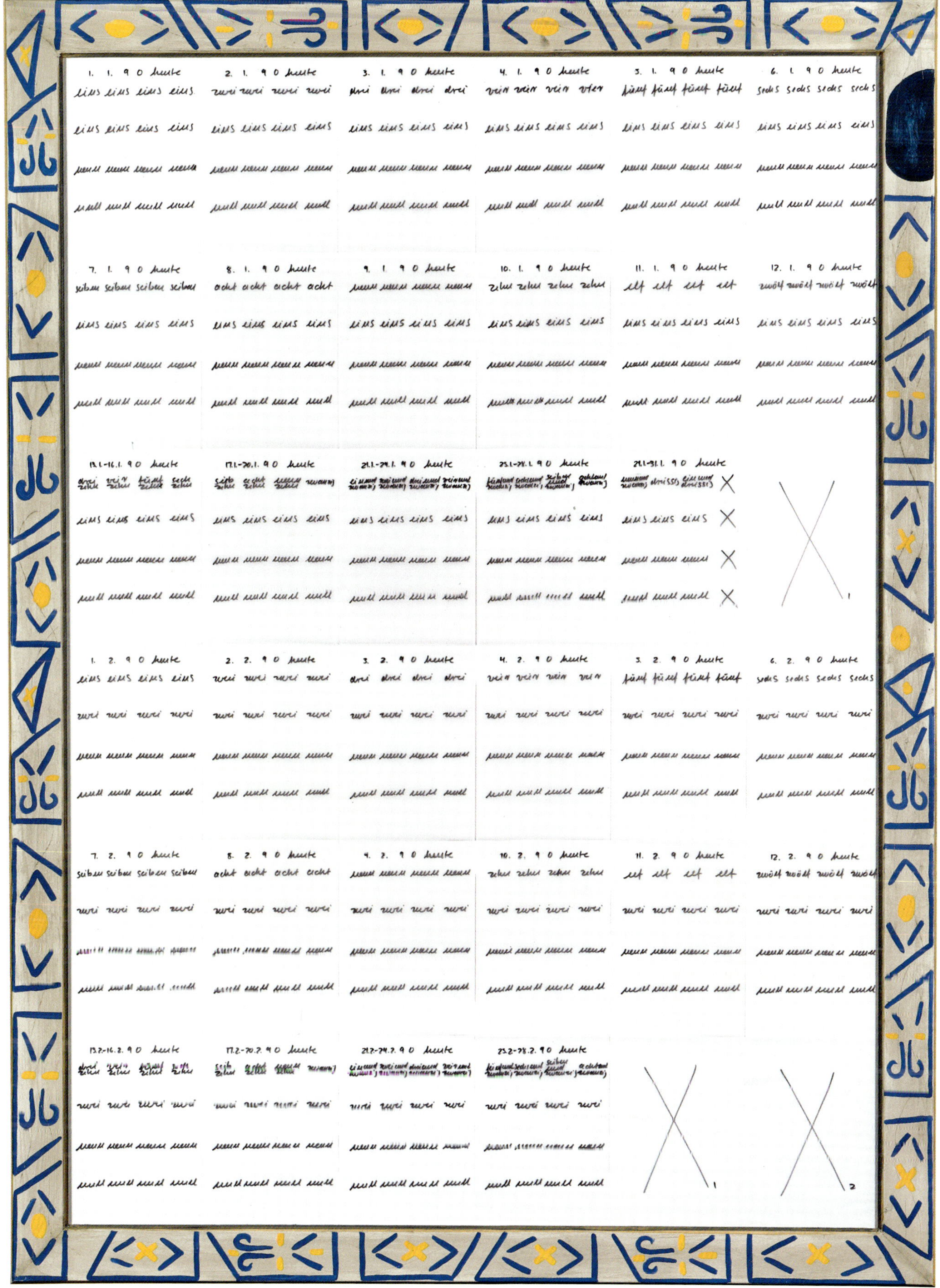

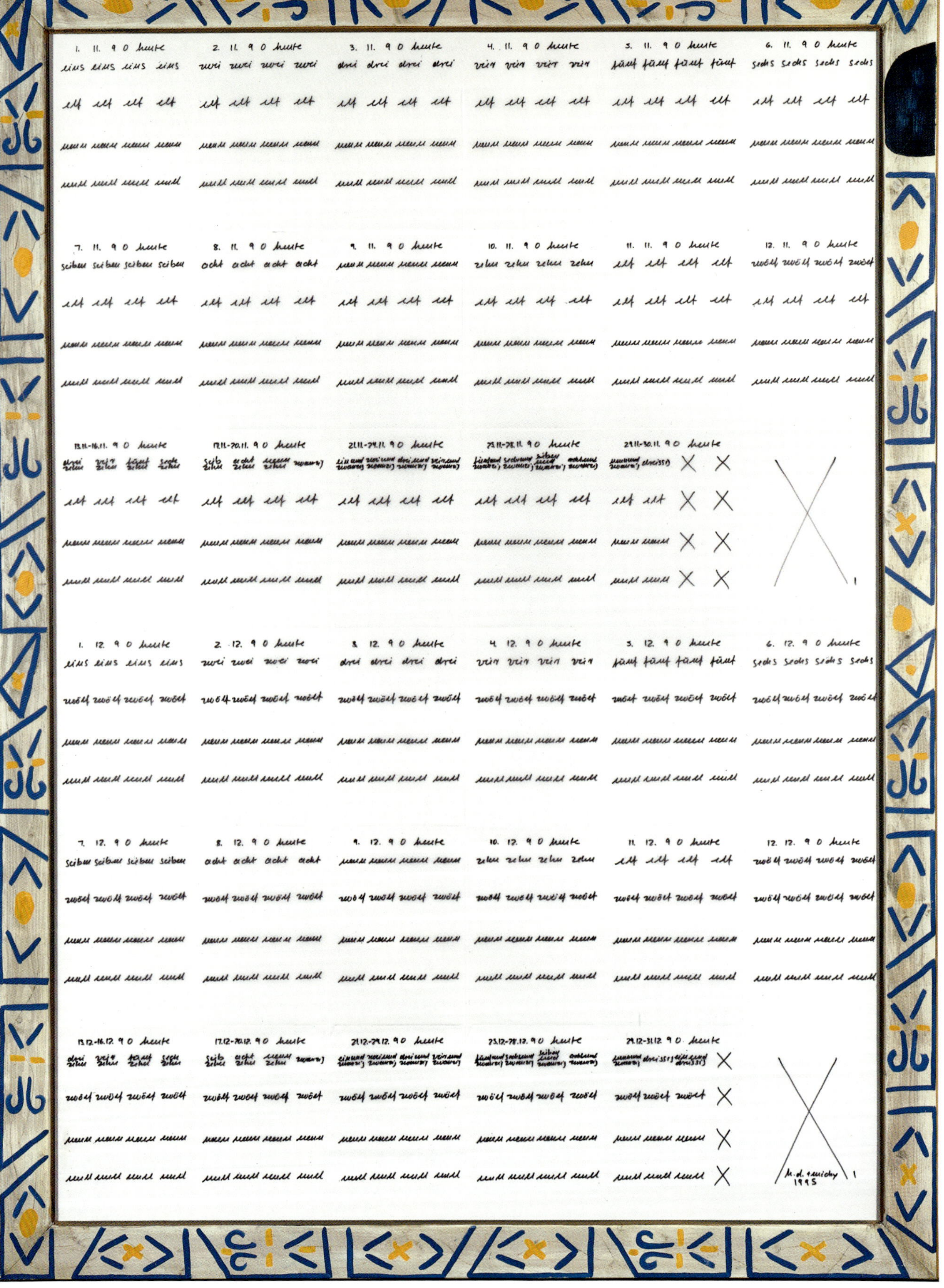

The Rehearsal of Hanne Darboven's Opus 60

Svenja Gräfin von Reichenbach

It was during one of the earliest discussions with Hanne Darboven about this commission that she announced that in addition to her numeric panels, the Picasso lithograph, and the sculptures that constitute *Hommage à Picasso*, she was in the process of preparing one last and new element for the installation: Opus 60. She offered no specific details about this unexpected dimension of the work. Over the course of the year or so between this conversation and the opening of the exhibition of the commission at Deutsche Guggenheim, her score was completed, transcribed into musical notations, and recorded by the Junge Sinfonie Berlin.

Hanne Darboven's Opus 60 is a challenge. It's not a solo, not a quartet, not a sextet, but rather it is a symphony with 120 players. The ensemble is larger than that required for most standard orchestral works with the exception of the great symphonies by Bruckner, Mahler, and Strauss. Moreover, Opus 60 has a highly unusual score, which can be read and interpreted in different ways, and which results in an unexpected sound, reflecting the fact that this music was not created in a traditional manner.

On August 11, 2005, 120 musicians from the Junge Sinfonie Berlin,[1] along with conductor Aurélien Bello,[2] gathered in the Berlin-Brandenburg Broadcasting Corporation's (RBB) television center in Berlin to rehearse Opus 60 before recording it on CD. The Ferenc-Fricsay Hall was filled with chairs, instrument cases, and an air of expectancy. The players asked questions about the music, some betraying a certain skepticism, and discussed the unusual composition and its musical notation. Throughout the rehearsal, it was impossible for the musicians to remain aloof from the proceedings. Opus 60 was forcing them into unknown territory, and they were eager to come to grips with this strange music and to understand who and what was behind it.

Hanne Darboven arrived on the 12:13 train from Hamburg and came straight to the rehearsal. You could see the intense concentration with which she greeted the first sounds of her new work. Completely absorbed in the music, she sat to one side of the room, listening to the imposing tutti alternating with filigree passages, which were more reminiscent of chamber music. The orchestra played one segment after another, rehearsing their endings again and again and repeating whole sections. Later Hanne Darboven would say, "The

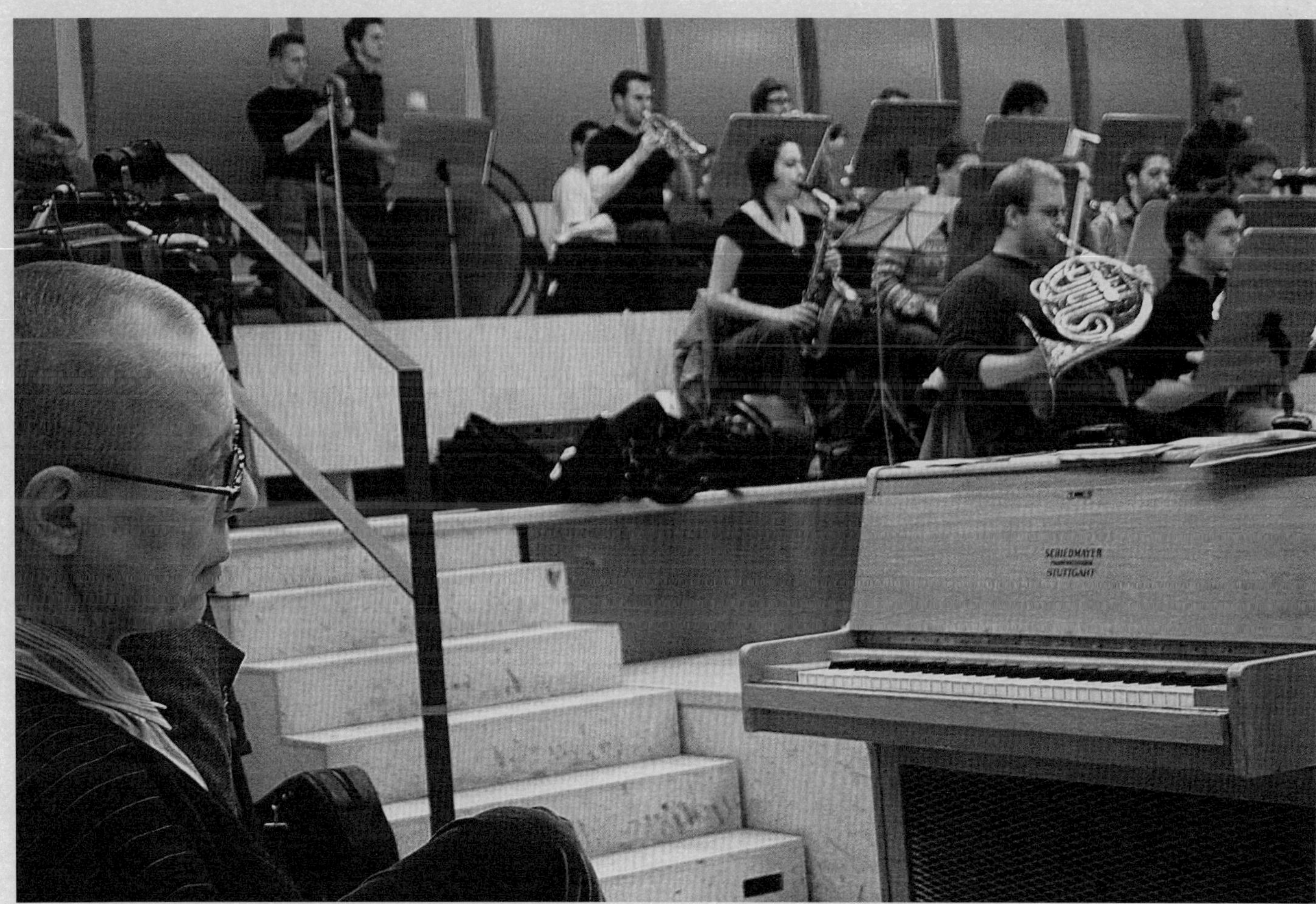

HANNE DARBOVEN ATTENDS THE REHEARSAL OF OPUS 60, AUGUST 2005

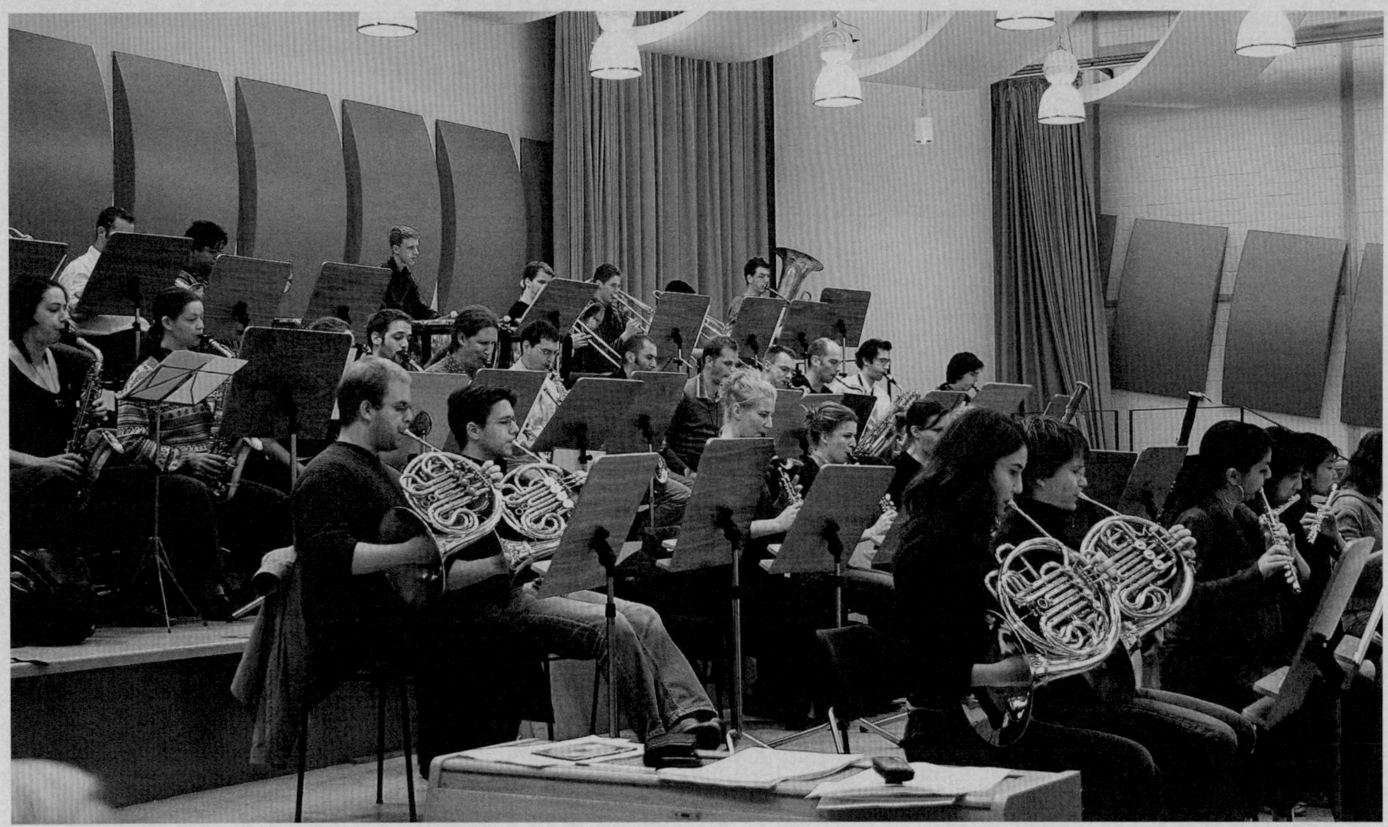

JUNGE SINFONIE BERLIN REHEARSES HANNE DARBOVEN'S OPUS 60, AUGUST 2005

musicians really got into it."[3] At the rehearsal's conclusion, the composer, visibly moved by what she had heard, stepped up onto the conductor's podium and thanked the musicians. Thanks were directed back at Darboven in the form of enthusiastic applause.

With the successful rehearsal behind them, the musicians eagerly showed up at Berlin's Teldex Studios the following day to record the CD. For the Junge Sinfonie Berlin, Opus 60 had become a communal experience, because unlike most orchestral works, for which each musician can practice his or her part ahead of time, this piece can only be worked out by the whole ensemble.[4] The orchestra approached the thirty-section composition theoretically, interpreting it in terms of Darboven's preoccupation with the phenomenon of time so that each of the thirty sections became a different day and the entire piece became a month. As the orchestra's manager Othmar Gimpel explained, "Opus 60 is a work that must be understood not simply as music but also as idea."

Since August 11, mementos of the Junge Sinfonie Berlin's dress rehearsal have found their way to Hanne Darboven's house in Burgberg. Framed photographs documenting the event now proudly decorate the walls and ceiling of her foyer.

Notes

1   The Junge Sinfonie Berlin plays a wide-ranging program, featuring twentieth-century orchestral works, as well as the classical repertory and the great concert literature of the Romantic era. In its more than fifteen years of performing, it has played works by Berg, Dallapiccola, Mahler, Shostakovich, Stravinsky, and Webern, among others.
2   Since December 2004, Aurélien Bello (b. 1980) has served as assistant conductor of the Junge Sinfonie Berlin. An accomplished harpist, he has toured with Claudio Abbado, Pierre Boulez, and others.
3   Hanne Darboven, conversation with the author, October 11, 2005, in Burgberg.
4   The Junge Sinfonie Berlin interpreted the work anew on February 3, 2006, at the Deutsche Bank Unter den Linden, Berlin, on the occasion of the opening of the exhibition *Hommage à Picasso*.

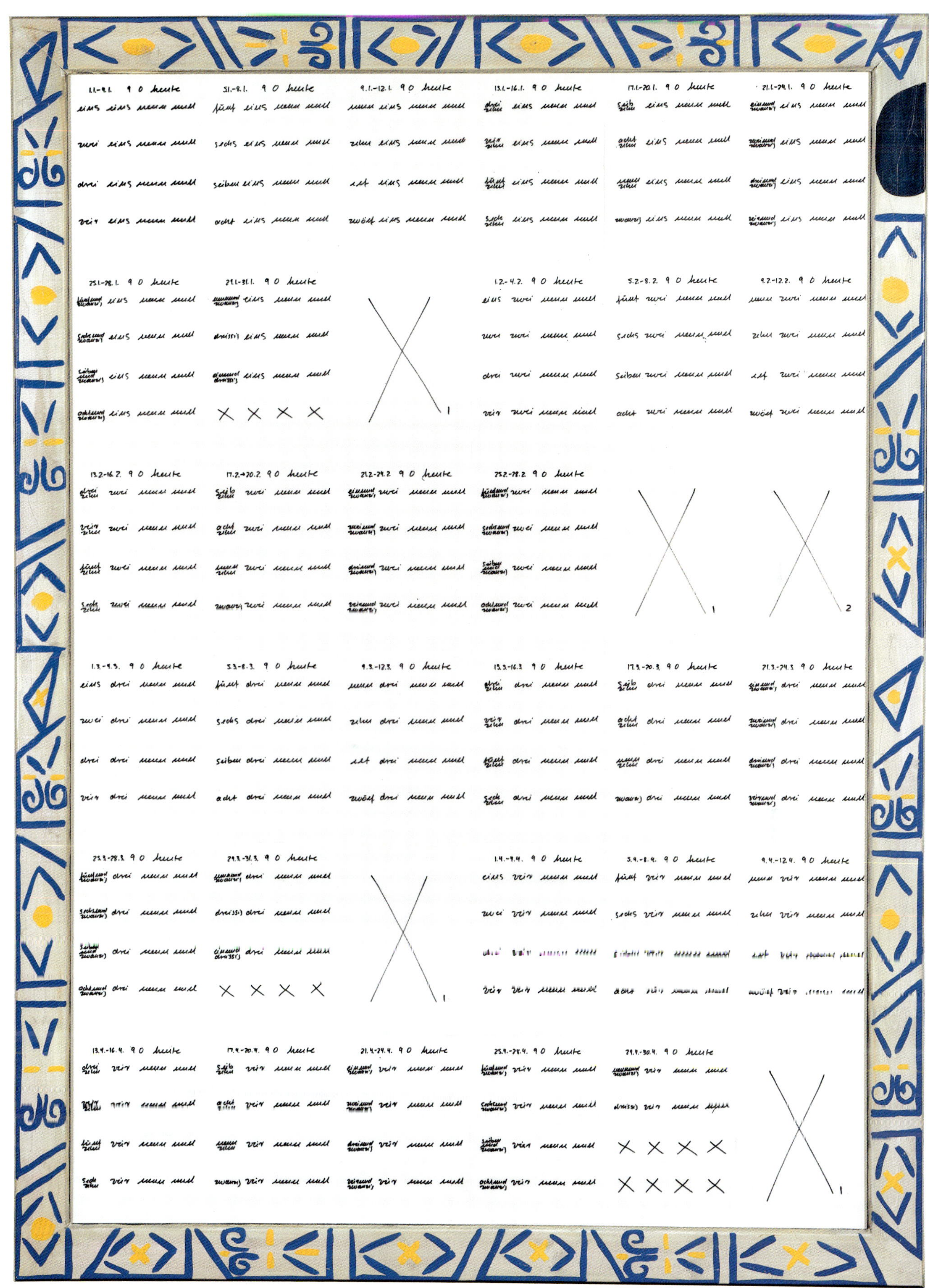

Framed text panels, from Hanne Darboven, *Hommage à Picasso*, 1995–2006. Felt-tip pen on parchment paper in painted wooden frames, 196.5 × 144 cm each panel, 36 sheets per panel, 30 × 21 cm each sheet.

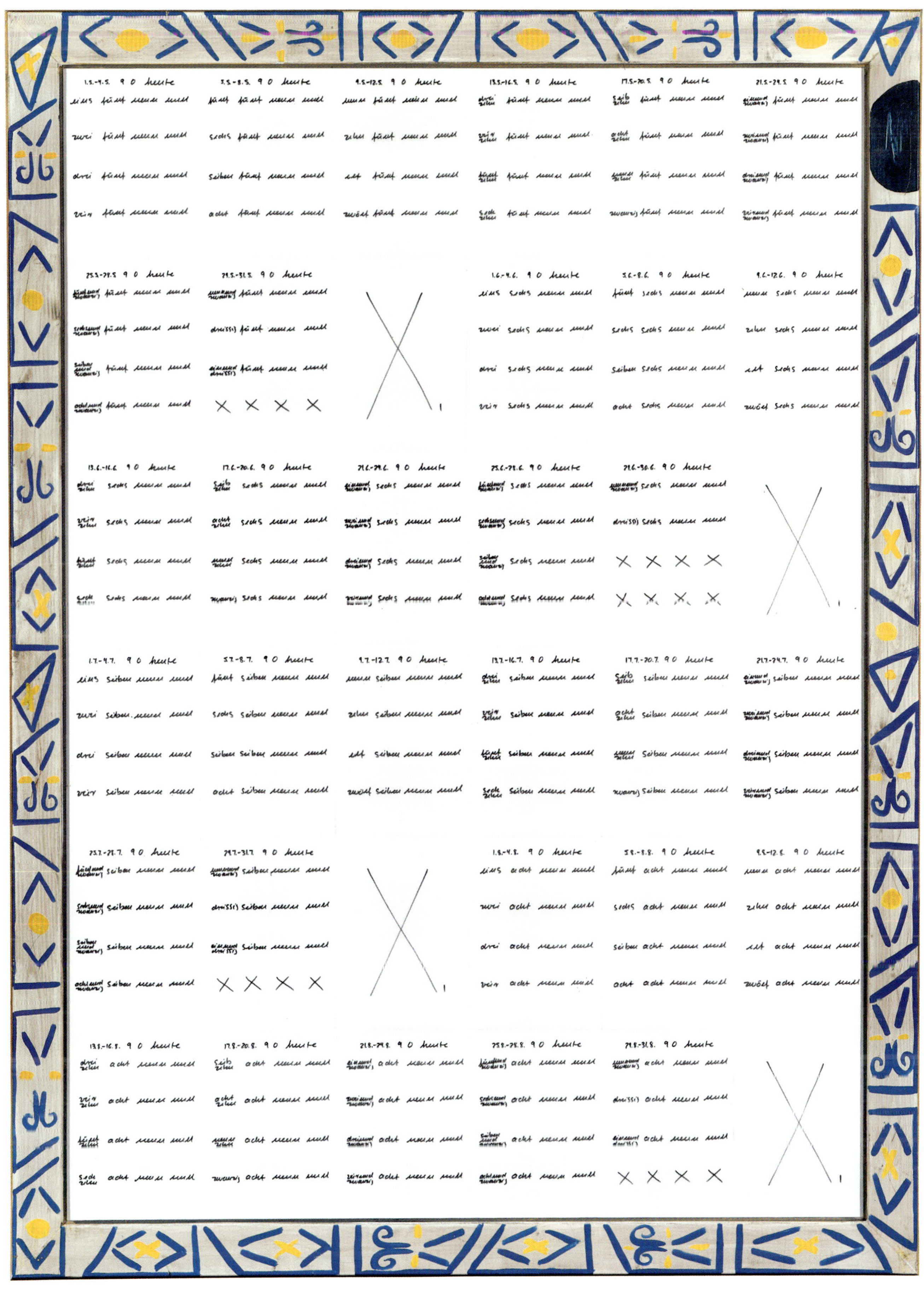

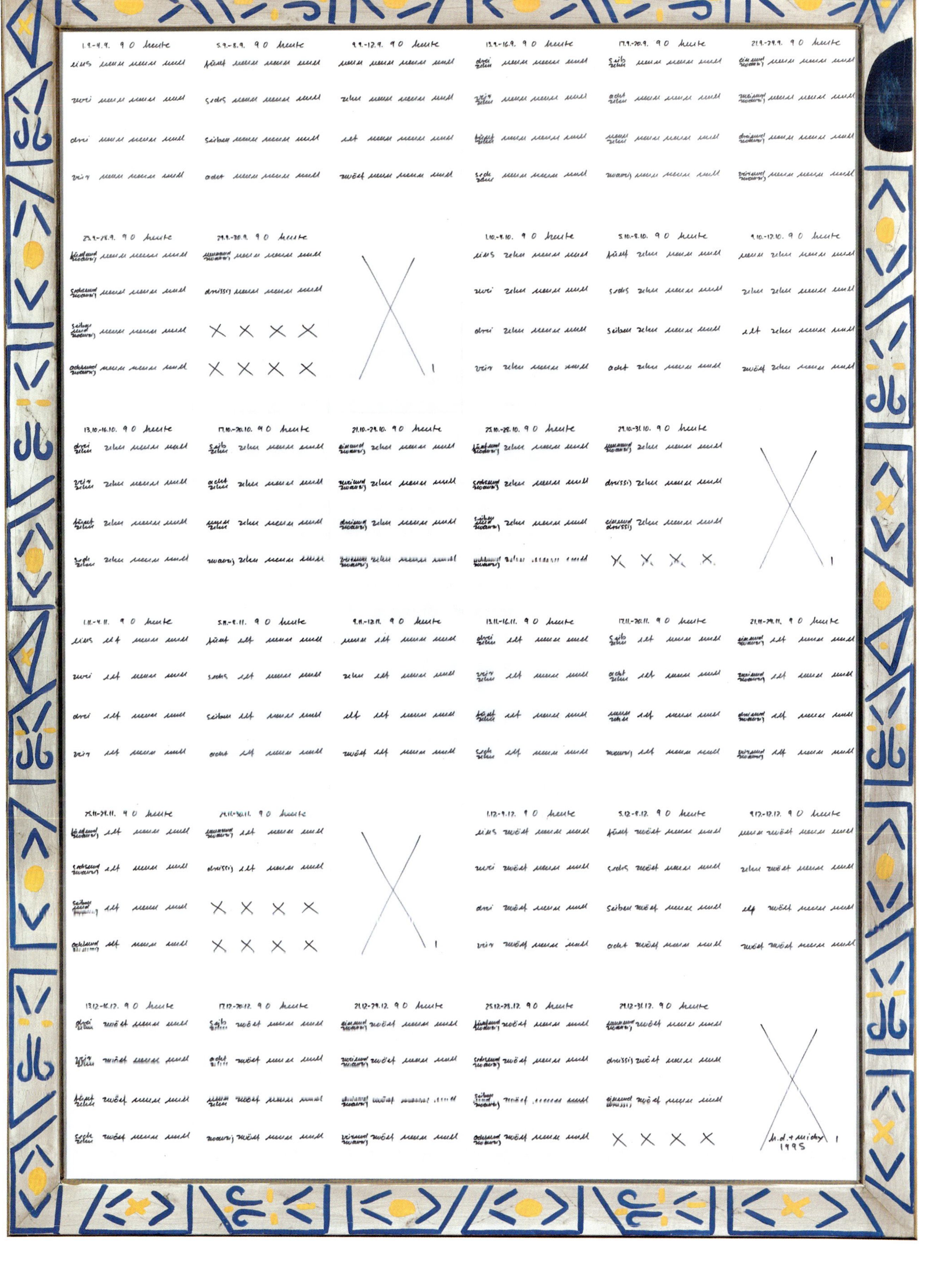

Selected Bibliography

1968

Darboven, Hanne. [Statement in] "Artists on Their Art." *Art International* 12, no. 4 (April 20, 1968), p. 55.

1969

Hanne Darboven. Exh. cat. Mönchengladbach: Städtisches Museum Abteiberg, 1969. With an essay by Johannes Cladders.

"Hanne Darboven: 6 Manuskripte '69'," *Kunst-Zeitung* 3 (July 1969). With text by Johannes Cladders.

Millet, Catherine. "L'Art Conceptuel." *Opus International*, no. 15. Paris: Editions Georges Fall, December 1969.

Konzeption/Conception. Exh. cat. Leverkusen: Städtisches Museum, 1969.

Szeemann, Harald. *Live in Your Head: When Attitudes Become Form: Works—Concepts—Processes—Situations—Information; Wenn Attitüden Form werden: Werke—Konzepte—Prozesse—Situationen—Information*. Exh. cat. Bern: Kunsthalle Bern, 1969.

1970

McShine, Kynaston L. *Information*. Exh. cat. New York: The Museum of Modern Art, 1970.

1971

Darboven, Hanne. *Ein Jahrhundert in einem Jahr*. Amsterdam: Stichting-Octopus; Düsseldorf: Galerie Konrad Fischer, 1971.

Fry, Edward F., and Diane Waldman. *Guggenheim International Exhibition*. Exh. cat. New York: Solomon R. Guggenheim Museum, 1971.

1972

Darboven, Hanne. "Words." *Avalanche*, no. 4 (spring 1972), pp. 42–51.

Szeemann, Harald, ed. *documenta 5: Befragung der Realität—Bildwelten heute*. Exh. cat. Kassel: Documenta GmbH, 1972.

Thwaites, John Anthony. "The Numbers Game." *Art and Artists* 6, no. 10 (January 1972), pp. 24–25.

1973

Darboven, Hanne. *El Lissitzki. K. und Pangeometrie*. Brussels: Daled & Gevaert; Société des Expositions du Palais des Beaux-Arts; Hamburg: Hossmann, 1973.

Darboven, Hanne. "Information." Milan: Flash Art Edizioni, 1973.

Lippard, Lucy. "Hanne Darboven: Deep in Numbers." *Artforum* 12, no. 2 (October 1973), pp. 35–39.

1974

Darboven, Hanne. *Hanne Darboven: Diary NYC February 15 until March 4 1974*. New York: Castelli Graphics; Turin: Gian Enzo Sperone, 1974.

Licht, Jennifer. *Eight Contemporary Artists*. Exh. cat. New York: The Museum of Modern Art, 1974. With text by Hanne Darboven.

Meyer, Franz, ed. *Ein Monat, ein Jahr, ein Jahrhundert. Werke von 1968 bis 1974*. Exh. cat. Basel: Kunstmuseum Basel, 1974; Amsterdam: Stedelijk Museum, 1975.

1976

Darboven, Hanne. *e.t.c. 2 = 1, 2; 1 + 1 = 1, 2*. Hamburg: Hanne Darboven, 1976.

Rose, Bernice. *Drawing Now*. Exh. cat. New York: The Museum of Modern Art, 1976.

1978

D'Amore, B. "Uso e abuso delle matematiche nelle arti visivem II." *D'Ars* 19, no. 87 (July 1978), pp. 22–39.

Lawson, Thomas. "Hanne Darboven at Castelli and Sperone Westwater Fischer." *Art in America* 66, no. 5 (September–October 1978), p. 117.

1979

Burgbacher-Krupka, Ingrid. *Strukturen zeitgenössischer Kunst. Eine empirische Untersuchung zur Rezeption der Werke von Beuys, Darboven, Flavin, Long, Walther*. Stuttgart: Enke, 1979.

Darboven, Hanne. *Bismarckzeit*. Cologne: Rheinland Verlag, 1979.

Honnef, Klaus. *Hanne Darboven: Bismarckzeit*. Exh. cat. Bonn: Rheinisches Landesmuseum, 1979.

1980

Darboven, Hanne. *Milieu >80<: heute. Freiheit statt Strauss. Friede statt Krieg*. Hamburg: Hanne Darboven, 1980.

Kuspit, Donald. "System as Desire: Hanne Darboven," *Art in America* 68, no. 6 (summer 1980), pp. 118–19.

1981

Haase, Amine. *Gespräche mit Künstlern*. Cologne: Wienand Verlag, 1981.

1982

Ammann, Jean Christophe, and C. Sauer, eds. *Werke aus der Sammlung Crex*. Exh. cat. Basel: Kunsthalle Basel, 1982.

Cladders, Johannes, ed. *Hanne Darboven: Pavilion of the FRG, Venice Biennale*. Exh. cat. Mönchengladbach: Städtisches Museum Abteiberg, 1982.

Darboven, Hanne. *"Schreibzeit", J. Cladders et H. Darboven*. Venice: Venice Biennale, 1982.

Hanne Darboven: Wende >80<. Exh. cat. Bonn: Bonner Kunstverein, 1982. With texts by Johannes Fritsch and Margarethe Jochimsen.

1983

Pohlen, Annelie. "Hanne Darboven's Time: The Content of Consciousness." *Artforum* 21, no. 8 (April 1983), pp. 52–53.

1985

L'oeil musicien: Les écritures et les images de la musique. Exh. cat. Charleroi, Belgium: Palais des Beaux-Arts, 1985.

1986

Bordaz, Jean-Pierre. "Hanne Darboven, or the Dimension of Time and Culture." *Parkett*, no. 10 (September 1986), pp. 109–11.

Pagé, Suzanne, ed. *Hanne Darboven: Histoire de la Culture, 1880-1983*. Exh. cat. Paris: Musée d'Art Moderne de la Ville de Paris, 1986.

1988

Froment, Jean-Louis, and Michel Bourel. *Art conceptuel I*. Exh. cat. Bordeaux: CAPC Musée d'Art Contemporain, 1988.

Hanne Darboven: Für Rainer Werner Fassbinder. Exh. cat. Munich: Kunstraum München, 1988.

1989

Faust, Wolfgang Max. "Hanne Darboven: Existenz." *Wolkenkratzer Art Journal*, no. 5 (September–October 1989), pp. 34–39.

Gintz, Claude. *L'art conceptuel: Une perspective*. Exh. cat. Paris: Musée d'Art Moderne de la Ville de Paris, 1989. With essays by Benjamin H. D. Buchloh, Gabriele Guercio, Charles Harrison, Robert C. Morgan, and Seth Siegelaub.

1990

Blase, Christoph. "Hanne Darbovens grosse Arbeit >Quartett '88<." *Kunst-Bulletin* (May 1990), pp. 34–35.

Block, René. *The Readymade Boomerang: Certain Relations in Twentieth Century Art*. Exh. cat. Sydney: Biennale of Sydney, 1990. With essays by Lynne Cooke, Anne Marie Freybourg, Dick Higgins, Bernice Murphy, and Emmett Williams.

Hanne Darboven. Edited by Gerd de Vries. Tokyo: Kyoto Shoin, 1990.

Graw, Isabelle. "Marking Time and Writing in the Work of Hanne Darboven." *Artscribe International*, no. 79 (January–February–March 1990), pp. 68–71.

Hanne Darboven: Primitive Zeit/Uhrzeit, Primitive Time/Clock Time. Exh. cat. Philadelphia: Goldie Paley Gallery, Moore College of Art and Design, 1990. With texts by Coosje van Bruggen, Klaus Honnef, and Elsa Longhauser, and an interview by Amine Haase.

Hanne Darboven: Quartett '88. Cologne: Walter König, 1990.

Koether, Jutta. "Hanne Darboven at Paul Maenz." *Flash Art*, no. 186 (February–March 1990), p. 138.

1991

Evolution >86<. Exh. cat. Munich: Staatsgalerie moderner Kunst, 1991.

Hanne Darboven: Die geflügelte Erde, Requiem. Exh. cat. Hamburg: Deichtorhallen Hamburg; Ostfildern: Cantz, 1991. With introduction by Zdenek Felix.

1994

Burgbacher-Krupka, Ingrid. *Hanne Darboven. Konstruiert, Literarisch, Musikalisch/ Constructed, Literary, Musical: The Sculpting of Time*. Exh. cat. Ostfildern: Cantz, 1994.

1995

Darboven, Hanne. *The Sculpting of Time*. Ostfildern: Cantz, 1995.

Goldstein, Ann, and Anne Rorimer. *Reconsidering the Object of Art: 1965–1975*. Exh. cat. Los Angeles: The Museum of Contemporary Art; Cambridge, Mass.: MIT Press, 1995. With essays by Susan L. Jenkins, Lucy Lippard, Stephen Melville, and Jeff Wall.

Karmel, Pepe. "Art in Review: Hanne Darboven." *New York Times*, September 19, 1995.

1997

Conzen, Ina. *Hanne Darboven: Kinder dieser Welt*. Exh. cat. Stuttgart: Staatsgalerie Stuttgart; Ostfildern: Cantz, 1997. With essay by Reinhard Ermen.

Sedofsky, Lauren. "Hanne Darboven: Dia Center for the Arts." *Artforum* 35, no. 7 (March 1997), pp. 88–89.

1998

Deep Storage: Collecting, Storing, and Archiving in Art. Exh. cat. Edited by Ingrid Schaffner and Matthias Winzen. Munich; New York: Prestel, 1998. With essay by Kai-Uwe Hemken.

Johnson, Ken. "Art in Review: Hanne Darboven." *New York Times*, January 23, 1998.

1999

Darboven, Hanne. *Ein Reader*. Cologne: Oktagon, 1999

Darboven, Hanne. "Catalogue for the concert . . . on April 28, 1999, in Berlin, and May 4, 1999, in Bonn." Edited by Ingrid Buschmann, Gabriele Knapstein, and Gerd de Vries. Berlin: Nationalgalerie im Hamburger Bahnhof—Museum für Gegenwart; Bonn: Kunst-und Ausstellungshalle der Bundesrepublik Deutschland; 1999.

Hanne Darboven. Das Frühwerk. Exh. cat. Hamburg: Hamburger Kunsthalle, 1999.

Hanne Darboven: Ein Jahrhundert—Johann Wolfgang von Goethe gewidmet =A Century—Dedicated to Johann Wolfgang von Goethe. Frankfurt am Main: Museum für Moderne Kunst, 1999.

Hanne Darboven: Menschen und Landschaften: In den Hallen für neue Kunst, Schaffhausen. Exh. cat. Hamburg: Christians, 1999.

2000

Darboven, Hanne. *Schreibzeit*. Cologne: Walter König, 2000. With texts by Bernhard Jussen, Laurenz Lütteken, Gerd de Vries, Otto Gerhard Oexle, and Ernst A. Busche.

Hanne Darboven/John Cage. Ostfildern: Cantz, 2000.

2001

Rorimer, Anne. *New Art in the 60s and 70s: Redefining Reality*. London: Thames & Hudson, 2001.

Women Artists in the Twentieth and Twenty-First Century. Edited by Uta Grosenick. Cologne; London: Taschen, 2001.

2002

Darboven, Hanne. *Kommentiertes Werkverzeichnis der Bücher*. Cologne: Walter König, 2002. With texts by Elke Bippus and Ortrud Westheider.

documenta 11. Exh. cat Ostfildern: Cantz, 2002.

Hanne Darboven: Kulturgeschichte 1880–1983. Cologne: Walter König; Ostfildern: Cantz, 2002.

Heartney, Eleanor. "A 600-Hour Documenta." *Art in America* 90, no. 9 (September 2002), pp. 86–95.

2003

Omlin, Sibylle. "My Work Ends in Music: Hanne Darboven's Notations as Musical Works." *Parkett*, no. 67 (May 2003), pp. 122–29.

2004

Hanne Darboven: Ein Jahrhundert-ABC. Exh. cat. Hannover: Kestnergesellschaft, 2004. With texts by Harald Falckenberg, Veit Görner, Sol LeWitt, Maik Schlüter, and Lawrence Weiner.

Newman, Michael. "Remembering and Repeating: Hanne Darboven's Work." In *Robert Lehman Lectures on Contemporary Art*. Edited by Lynne Cooke and Karen Kelly with Betinna Funcke. New York: Dia Art Foundation, 2004.

2005

Garrels, Gary. *Drawing from the Modern, 1945–1975*. Exh. cat. New York: The Museum of Modern Art, 2005.

Solo Exhibitions

1967-68
Konrad Fischer Galerie, Düsseldorf, *Hanne Darboven: Konstruktionen-Zeichnungen*, December 5–January 2.

1969
Städtisches Museum, Mönchengladbach, West Germany, *Hanne Darboven: Ausstellung mit 6 Filmprojektoren nach 6 Büchern über 1968*, February 25–April 7.

1971
Konrad Fischer Galerie, Düsseldorf, *Ein Jahrhundert in einem Jahr*, January 1–December 31.

Westfälischer Kunstverein, Münster, West Germany, *Hanne Darboven*, October 16–November 14.

1972
Kunstmuseum Luzern, Switzerland, in cooperation with Gian Enzo Sperone, Turin, *Hanne Darboven*, May 11–June 22.

1974
Kabinett für aktuelle Kunst, Bremerhaven, West Germany, *Zeichnungen*, January 12–February 10.

Castelli Graphics, New York, *Hanne Darboven: Diary N.Y.C. February 15 until March 4, 1974*, February 15–March 4. Other venue: Gian Enzo Sperone, Turin.

Museum of Modern Art, Oxford, England, *Hanne Darboven*, June 30–August 4.

Kunstmuseum Basel, *Ein Monat, ein Jahr, ein Jahrhundert. Werke von 1968 bis 1974*. Other venue: Stedelijk Museum, Amsterdam.

1976
Leo Castelli, New York, *Hanne Darboven: For Jean-Paul Sartre*, May 1–22.

1979
Rheinisches Landesmuseum, Bonn, *Hanne Darboven: Bismarckzeit*.

1981
Leo Castelli, New York, *Hanne Darboven: Wende >80<*, November 21–December 19. Other venues: Galerie Konrad Fischer, Zurich; Bonner Kunstverein, Bonn; Gelbe Musik, Berlin; Rijksmuseum Kröller-Müller, Otterlo, Netherlands.

1983
Kunstverein Hamburg, *Schreibzeit*, January 29–February 27.

1985
Musée d'Art Moderne de la Ville de Paris, *Hanne Darboven: Histoire de la Culture, 1880-1983*, April 29–June 22.

1989
Galerie Paul Maenz, Cologne, *Hanne Darboven, Existenz*, September 16–October 4.

1989-90
Renaissance Society at the University of Chicago, *Hanne Darboven, Quartett >88<: Marie Curie, Rosa Luxemburg, Gertrude Stein, Virginia Woolf*, December 1–January 7. Other venues: Portikus, Frankfurt; Neue Gesellschaft für Bildende Kunst, Berlin; Museum of Contemporary Art, Los Angeles.

1990
Leo Castelli, New York, *Hanne Darboven: Requiem for M. Oppenheimer*, January 6–27.

Goldie Paley Gallery, Moore College of Art and Design, Philadelphia, *Hanne Darboven: Primitive Zeit/Uhrzeit, Primitive Time/Clock Time*, November 2–December 15.

1991
Kunsthalle Basel, *Hanne Darboven: Symphonie Fin de Siècle—Opus 27/ABC—Symphonie—Opus 37*, June 8–July 28.

Deichtorhallen Hamburg, *Hanne Darboven: Die geflügelte Erde, Requiem*, October 22–November 24. Other venue: Stedelijk Van Abbemuseum, Eindhoven, Netherlands.

Staatsgalerie moderner Kunst, Munich, *Evolution >86<*.

1993
Leo Castelli, New York, *Hanne Darboven: Twentieth Anniversary*, April 24–May 22.

Elisabeth Kaufmann, Basel, *Hanne Darboven: Editionen*, May–June.

1995
Institut für Auslandsbeziehungen, Stuttgart, *Wende >80</Kreuzfahrt zur Hölle*.

1996
Dia Center for the Arts, New York, *Hanne Darboven: Kulturgeschichte, 1880-1983*, March 28–June 1.

1997
Staatsgalerie Stuttgart, *Hanne Darboven: Kinder dieser Welt*, July 12–September 28.

1999
Nationalgalerie im Hamburger Bahnhof—Museum für Gegenwart, Berlin, *Musikwerke Bildender Künstler*, April 28. Other venue: Kunst- und Ausstellungshalle der Bundesrepublik Deutschland, Bonn, May 4.

Busch-Reisinger Museum, Harvard University Art Museums, Cambridge, Massachusetts, *Hanne Darboven, 1969/1972/1983*, September 4–November 7.

1999-2000
Hamburger Kunsthalle, Hamburg, *Hanne Darboven. Das Frühwerk*, October 29–February 13.

Deichtorhallen Hamburg, *Hommage à Picasso*, November 19–February 27.

2000
Schaffhausen, Hallen für neue Kunst, Switzerland, *Menschen und Landschaften*, May–October.

2002
Westfälisches Landesmuseum, Münster, Germany, *Hanne Darboven, Bücher 1966-2002*, March 24–May 26.

2004
Kestnergesellschaft, Hannover, *Hanne Darboven, Ein Jahrhundert–ABC*, March 28–June 27.

2005
Klemens Gasser & Tanja Grunert, New York, *Hanne Darboven*, September 9–October 8.

Group Exhibitions

1967
Lannis Museum of Normal Art, New York, *Normal Art*.

1969
Neue Nationalgalerie, Berlin, *Sammlung 1968: Karl Ströher*, April 25–June 17. Other venues: Kunsthalle Düsseldorf; Kunsthalle Bern, Switzerland.

Städtisches Museum, Leverkusen, *Konzeption/Conception*, October 24–November 23.

Kunsthalle Bern, Switzerland, *Live in Your Head: When Attitudes Become Form: Works—Concepts—Processes—Situations*. Other venues: Museum Haus Lange, Krefeld, West Germany; Institute of Contemporary Arts, London.

1970
Galleria civica d'arte moderna, Turin, *Conceptual Art, Arte Povera, Land Art*, June–July.

The Museum of Modern Art, New York, *Information*, July 2–September 20.

1971
Solomon R. Guggenheim Museum, New York, *Guggenheim International Exhibition*, February 12–April 11.

Septième Biennale de Paris, September 24–November 1.

1972
Kunstmuseum Basel, *'Konzept'-Kunst*, March 18–April 23.

documenta 5, Kassel, June 30–October 8.

1973
Duodécimo Bienal de São Paulo, Brazil.

1974-75
The Museum of Modern Art, New York, *Eight Contemporary Artists*, October 9–January 5.

1975
Rijksmuseum Kröller-Müller, Otterlo, Netherlands, *Functions of Drawings*, May 25–August 4.

1976
The Museum of Modern Art, New York, *Drawing Now*, January 19–March 7. Traveled under the auspices of the International Council of the Museum of Modern Art.

1977
The Art Institute of Chicago, *Europe in the Seventies: Aspects of Recent Art*. March 16–May 7. Other venues: Hirshhorn Museum and Sculpture Garden, Smithsonian Institution, Washington, D.C.; Museum of Modern Art, San Francisco; The Fort Worth Art Museum, Texas; The Contemporary Arts Center, Cincinnati.

documenta 6, Kassel, June 24–October 2.

1979
Art Gallery of New South Wales, Sydney, *The Third Biennale of Sydney: European Dialogue*, April 12–May 27.

1981
Musée d'Art Moderne de la Ville de Paris, *Art Allemagne/Aujourd'hui*, January 17–March 8.

1982
Stedelijk Museum, Amsterdam, *'60/'80 Attitudes, Concepts, Images*, April–July.

German Pavilion, *La Biennale di Venezia*, June–October.

documenta 7, Kassel, June 19–August 28.

1984–85
Hirshhorn Museum and Sculpture Garden, Smithsonian Institution, Washington, D.C., *Tenth Anniversary Exhibition*, October 4–January 6.

1985
Palais des Beaux-Arts, Charleroi, Belgium, *L'oeil musicien: Les écritures et les images de la musique*, March 28–May 12.

1987
Bonner Kunstverein, Bonn, *Wechselströme. Kontemplation, Expression, Konstruktion*, January 6–March 22.

1989
National Museum of Art, Osaka, *Drawing as Itself*, October 7–November 26.

1989–90
Musée d'Art Moderne de la Ville de Paris, *L'art conceptuel: Une perspective*, November 22–February 18.

1990
Art Gallery of New South Wales, Sydney, *Eighth Biennale of Sydney: The Readymade Boomerang*, April 11–June 3.

1992
Walker Art Center, Minneapolis, *Photography in Contemporary German Art, 1960 to the Present*, February 9–May 31. Other venues: Louisiana Museum of Modern Art, Humlebaek; Museum Ludwig, Cologne; Guggenheim Museum SoHo, New York.

1994
Ydessa Hendeles Art Foundation, Toronto, *Chronicles*, May.

1995–96
The Museum of Contemporary Art, Los Angeles, *Reconsidering the Object of Art: 1965–1975*, October 15–February 4.

1997
Staatsgalerie Stuttgart, *Magie der Zahl in der Kunst des 20. Jahrhunderts*, February 1–March 19.

Martin-Gropius-Bau, Berlin, *Die Epoche der Moderne. Kunst im 20. Jahrhundert*, May 7–July 27.

Halle Tony Garnier, Lyon, *Quatrième Biennale de Lyon d'art contemporain*, July 9–September 24.

Haus der Kunst, Munich, *Deep Storage: Arsenale der Erinnerung*, August 3–October 12. Other venues: Sonderausstellungshalle am Kulturforum, Berlin; Kunstmuseum Düsseldorf im Ehrenhof; P.S. 1 Contemporary Art Center, New York; Henry Art Gallery, Seattle.

1999
Museum Fridericianum, Kassel, *Chronos & Kairos: Die Zeit in der zeitgenössischen Kunst*, September 5–November 7.

P.S. 1 Contemporary Art Center, New York, *The Promise of Photography: Selected Works from the DG Bank Collection*, September 12–October 24.

1999–2000
Carnegie Museum of Art, Pittsburgh, *Carnegie International 1999/2000*, November 6–March 26.

2000
Kunstverein für die Rheinlande und Westfalen, Düsseldorf, *Kabinett der Zeichnung*, September 23–November 11. Other venues: Kunstverein Lingen Kunsthalle, Germany; Kunstsammlungen Chemnitz, Germany; Württembergischer Kunstverein Stuttgart.

2000–01
National Gallery, Prague, *Beyond Preconceptions: The Sixties Experiment*, November 2–January 14.

2002
documenta 11, Kassel, June 8–September 15.

2003
Museum Morsbroich, Leverkusen, Germany, *Talking Pieces—Text und Bild in der zeitgenössischen Kunst*, January 26–April 20

DaimlerChrysler Contemporary, Berlin, *Minimalism and After II*, February 2–June 18.

Städtische Galerie Erlangen, Germany, *Out of Print—Vergriffen*, August 9–September 28

2003–04
Neues Museum Weserburg, Bremen, Germany, *Die Bücher der Künstler*, November 1–February 22.

Haus der Kunst, Munich, *Partners*, November 7–February 15.

2004
Los Angeles County Museum of Art, *Beyond Geometry: Experiments in Form 1940s–70s*, June 13–October 3.

South African National Gallery, Cape Town, *DaimlerChrysler Collection for South Africa*, October 4–November 30. Other venues: Pretoria Art Museum; Museum Africa, Johannesburg.

2004–05
MUMOK, Vienna, *Minimal-, Concept-, Land Art und Arte Povera*, March 26–December 31

2005
ZKM Museum für Neue Kunst, Karlsruhe, Germany, *EXIT—AUSSTIEG AUS DEM BILD*, January 14–August 14.

Museum of Modern Art, New York, *Drawing from the Modern, 1945–1975*, March 30–August 29.

Konrad Fischer Galerie, Düsseldorf, *Hanne Darboven* (with Manfred Pernice), April 9–May 28.

Kunstsammlungen Chemnitz, Germany, *Schrift. Zeichen. Geste*, July 24–November 9.

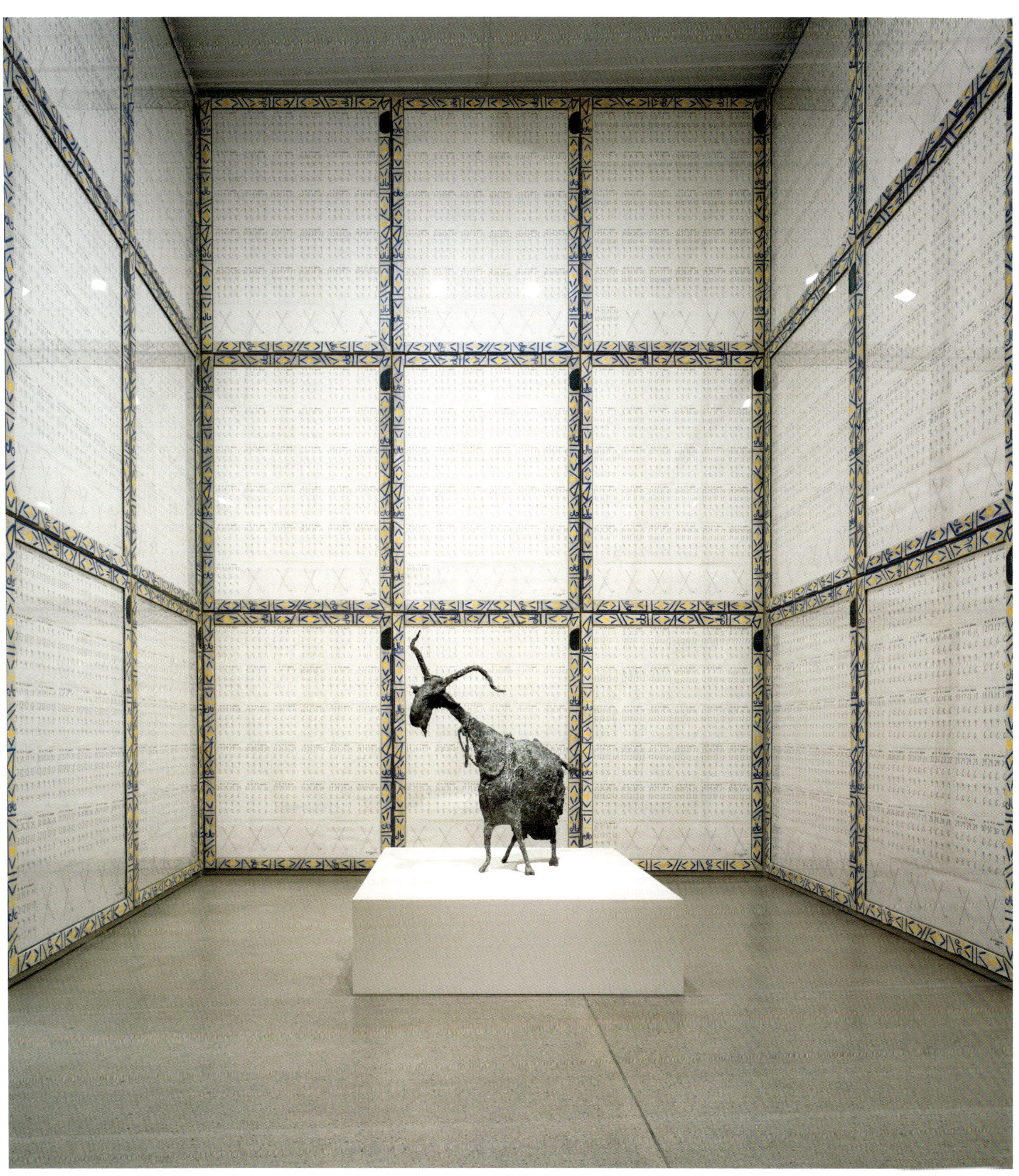

Above and reverse page:
Installation views of the exhibition
Hanne Darboven: Hommage à Picasso
Deutsche Guggenheim, Berlin, February
2006. Photos: Mathias Schormann

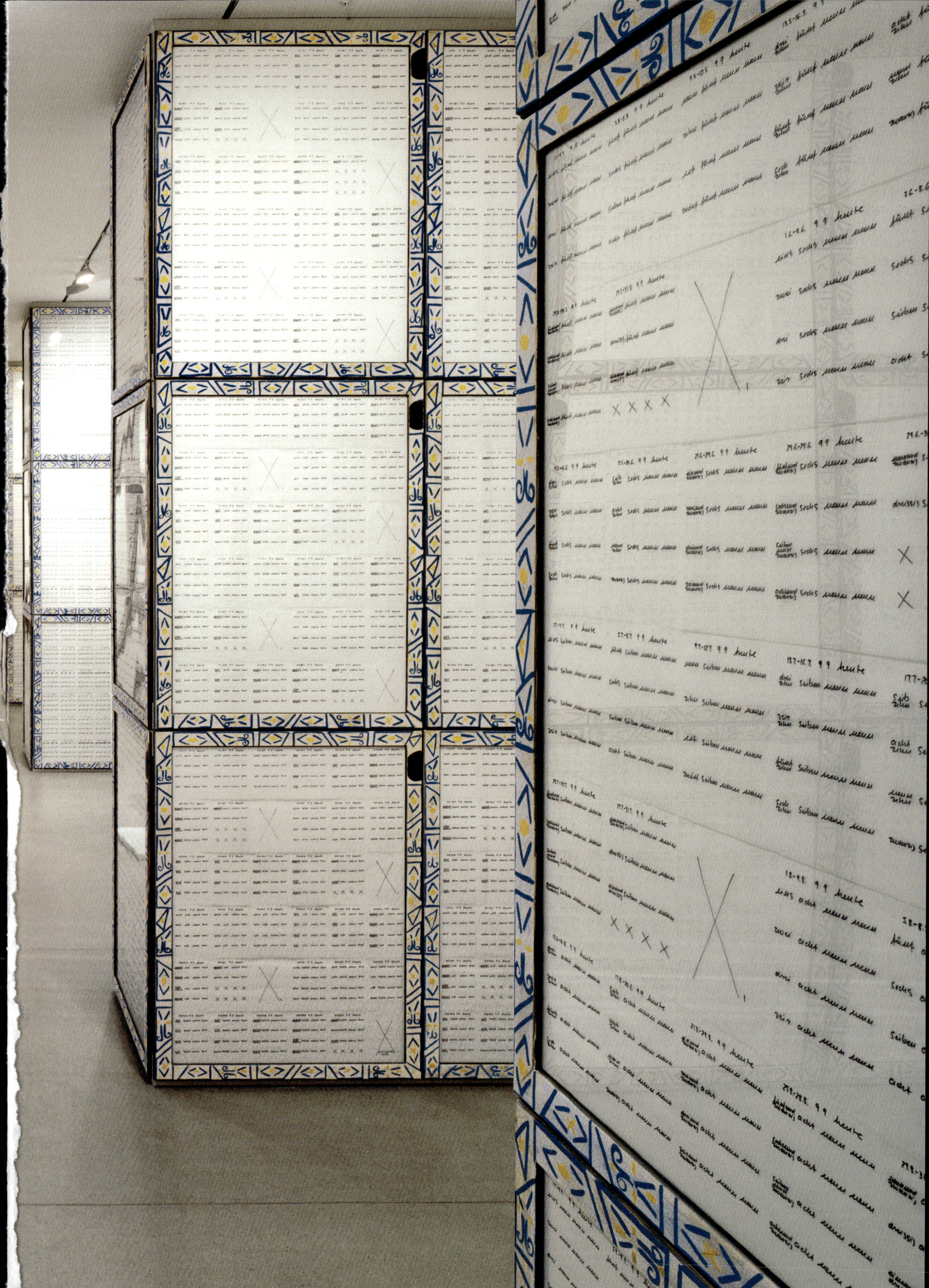

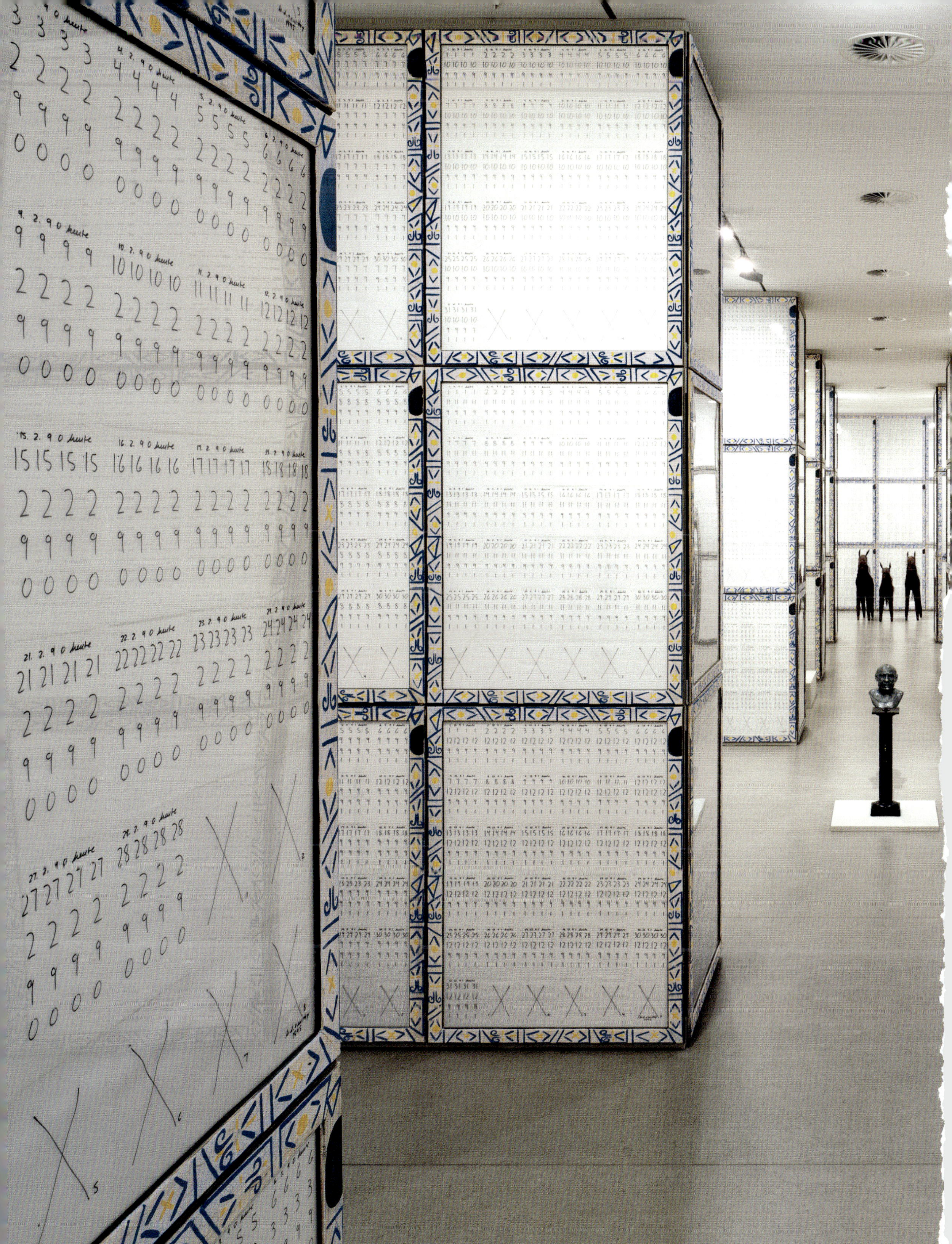

Hanne Darboven's *Hommage à Picasso* (1995–2006) is an installation comprising original works by Darboven and commissioned and purchased works by other artists and craftsmen. It includes:

Hanne Darboven, 270 framed text panels, 1995–96. Felt-tip pen on parchment paper in painted wooden frames, 196.5 x 144 cm each panel, 36 sheets per panel, 30 x 21 cm each sheet;

Hanne Darboven, Symphony for 120 Instruments, Opus 60 (with Epilogue: Intermezzo from Franz Schmidt's opera *Notre Dame* [1902–04], 00:04:30), 2003–06, 00:36:03 without Epilogue. First performance by the Junge Sinfonie Berlin (Conductor: Aurélien Bello), February 3, 2006, Deutsche Guggenheim, Berlin;

Framed reproduction of Pablo Picasso's *Seated Figure in Turkish Costume* (1955; Collection of Hamburger Kunsthalle), n.d. Lithograph in painted wooden frame, 99.2 x 82.5 cm;

Bust of Picasso, by Inge Polynice, 1999. Bronze, edition 2/8, 151 x 33.5 x 29 cm overall;

Goat, by Wolfgang Binding, 1994. Bronze, 120 x 124 x 42 cm;

Three donkeys, craftwork from Poland, n.d. Birch twigs, 169 x 143 x 43 cm, 196 x 173 x 45 cm, and 200 x 173 x 44 cm;

Twelve signs of the zodiac, by Meta Morfosi, 1992. Polished and patinated cast metal, with two vitrines with sculptural tops, 201.5 x 35 x 35 cm each vitrine without top; vitrine top with Sun with its planets, 101.5 x 64 x 57 cm; vitrine top with Earth and moon, 66 x 35 x 35 cm.